THE ART AND CRAFT OF
WOODCARVING

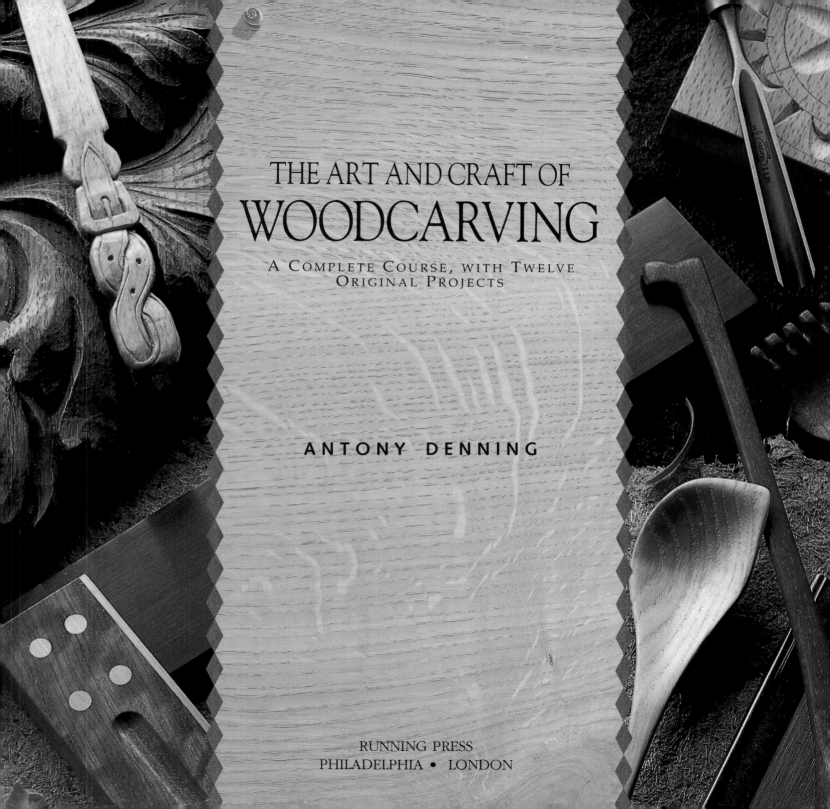

THE ART AND CRAFT OF
WOODCARVING

A Complete Course, with Twelve Original Projects

ANTONY DENNING

RUNNING PRESS

PHILADELPHIA • LONDON

A QUARTO BOOK

Copyright © 1994 Quarto Inc.

All rights reserved under the Pan American and
International Copyright Conventions. First published in the
United States of America in 1994 by Running Press Book
Publishers.

This book may not be reproduced in whole or in part in any
form or by any means, electronic or mechanical, including
photocopying, recording or by any information storage or
retrieval system now known or hereafter invented, without
written permission from the Publisher.

9 8 7 6 5 4 3 2 1

Digit on the right indicates the number of this printing

ISBN 1-56138-408-9

Library of Congress Cataloging-in-Publication Number:
93-87399

This book was designed and produced by
Quarto Inc.
6 Blundell Street
London N7 9BH

Senior editor Sally MacEachern
Editor Mary Senechal
Consultant editor Bob Flexner
Senior art editor Penny Cobb
Assistant art editor Penny Dawes
Designer Hugh Schermuly
Photographers Paul Forrester, Laura Wickenden, Les Weiss
Picture researcher Susannah Jayes
Illustrator Rob Shone
Picture manager Giulia Hetherington
Editorial director Sophie Collins
Art director Moira Clinch

Typeset by Central Southern Typesetters, Eastbourne
Manufactured by Eray Scan Pte Ltd, Singapore
Printed by Star Standard Industries (Pte) Ltd, Singapore

This book may be ordered by mail from the publisher. Please
include $2.50 for postage and handling. *But try your
bookstore first!*

Running Press Book Publishers
125 South Twenty-second Street
Philadelphia, Pennsylvania 19103-4399

PUBLISHER'S NOTE

Woodcarving can be dangerous. Before you
use any hand or power tools, read the safety
box on page 38. Always exercise caution and
read instructions carefully.

As far as the methods and techniques
mentioned in this book are concerned, all
statements, information, and advice given
here are believed to be accurate. However,
neither the author, copyright holder, nor the
publisher can accept any legal liability for
errors or omissions.

CONTENTS

PICTORIAL WOODCUT • 74

Objective: to gain more experience in using carving tools by making a woodcut that will produce an attractive print

LETTER OPENER • 82

Objective: to carve a letter opener with a subtle but effective pattern in low relief on the handle and a simply shaped blade

CHIP CARVING • 88

Objective: to become familiar with a different carving technique for which the traditional tools are knives but which can equally well be done with chisels

BOX OR TABLE LAMP • 94

Objective: to carve a simple design with a clean, flat, recessed background, suitable for a box or lamp base

LETTER CUTTING • 104

Objective: to become familiar with letter-cutting techniques by designing and carving a variety of letters. The result should be well-designed and easy to read

SPOONS AND SALAD UTENSILS • 114

Objective: to carve a pleasing functional object with a smooth transition from bowl to handle and a harmonious overall shape

BOWL WITH HANDLES • 124

Objective: to design and carve a bowl, relating the inside shape to the outside shape. The bowl may be decorated or left plain

RELIEF PANEL • 134

Objective: to carve a pictorial relief in realistic style with a plain background

MIRROR FRAME • 140

Objective: to design and carve a frame of simple construction with applied decoration that follows a pictorial theme

SIGNS OF THE ZODIAC • 152

Objective: to produce a decorative carving designed to appear three-dimensional, but intended for display against a wall

CARVING IN THREE DIMENSIONS • 160

Objective: to carve a fully three-dimensional piece, which is visually satisfying from all viewpoints

CARVED MASK • 166

Objective: to carve a deeply modeled head in high relief as a decorative object

INTRODUCTION

Woodcarving is an activity that spans the globe and the centuries. It embraces a huge variety of applications, from the creation of everyday objects and decorative patterns to architectural features and abstract sculptures. It can be an art or a craft – and it can be both.

Woodcarving uses tools to reveal a shape that exists in the wood and in the mind of the carver, which might be anything from a pattern on a bowl to a human form. The craft of carving is the acquired skill of removing the unwanted wood efficiently. There are carvers who excel at this, reproducing with speed and precision whatever they are asked to carve, but who would be unable to design and carve a piece of their own. There are others who excel in designing, but who would hesitate to carve a repeat pattern on molding. In between lies a great range of skills, where the balance gradually shifts from craft to sculpture. Carving, however, is not the preserve of the craftsman or artist, but an activity open to anyone who wants to work with wood.

The desire to carve appears to have been part of the human make-up since time began. All over the world, people of every culture and period have shaped figures and decorated objects and buildings with carved patterns, often producing brilliant work with the most primitive of tools. Carvings can have a profound religious or ritual significance. Like all art, they may be used for the display of wealth and power. But equally, carving often exists for purely esthetic reasons.

THE CARVING TRADITION

Our earliest ancestors were making carvings tens of thousands of years ago, as exemplified by Paleolithic figures such as the Venus of Willendorf and the Venus of Lespugne. If they carved mammoth ivory and reindeer antler, and engraved stone, how much easier it would have been for them to carve wood – and we may assume that they did. If we have no evidence for this assumption, it is hardly surprising: wood is vulnerable to attack by fungus, insects, and fire; to survive even a few centuries requires favorable conditions.

The ancient Egyptians left examples of carved furniture in their royal tombs, and at least one stool with carved legs survives from Hellenistic times (4th–1st century B.C.). Through the Dark Ages in Europe, however, the depredations of successive invaders probably destroyed a great deal. Valuables could be buried for

Wooden figure
The Nazca culture of south Peru flourished during the first millenium A.D.

safety, but a beautifully carved piece of furniture could not. Nevertheless, the carving tradition continued, particularly in churches. The exquisite carvings on Romanesque churches of 11th-12th century Scandinavia, for example, bear witness to the toleration of pagan Norse motifs on Christian churches. These Celtic designs of great complexity are akin to those in illuminated manuscripts.

Then, in the 15th and 16th centuries, came the great flowering of basswood carving in Germany, exemplified by such names as Tilman Riemenschneider (died 1531) and Veit Stoss (died 1533).

Attributed to Grinling Gibbons

This basswood overmantel is typical of Grinling Gibbons' ornate, delicate style.

Another great period of European carving occurred in the late 17th and 18th centuries with the work of carvers such as Grinling Gibbons (1648–1721), renowned for the delicacy of his carving in St. Paul's Cathedral in London and other churches and his embellishment of grand English homes. A gifted designer and decorative artist, he epitomized that middle ground where the art and the craft of woodcarving merge. Even in the 18th century, however, materials (such as carton pierre and composition) were being developed to replace the expensive work of the carver. Ironically, the molds for these materials had to be carved from very hard woods, such as apple or boxwood, with complicated designs worked in reverse by the very carvers who were doing themselves out of a job.

In the days before color printing, television, and widespread travel, people rarely saw creative work from other cultures; and if they did, they were unlikely to accept its validity in terms of their own art tradition. Trade did have some influence on the decorative arts – such as the fashion for chinoiserie in 18th-century Europe – but it did not alter the fundamental approach of the indigenous craftsman.

NEW WAYS OF SEEING

In the late 19th century, some European artists began to appreciate that the carvings brought back from distant lands were not mere curios made by primitive peoples, but works of art in their own right. This realization culminated in 1907 with the painting by Picasso (1881–1973) of "Les Demoiselles d'Avignon," the forerunner of cubism and a work which initially shocked many artists, let alone a wider audience. From that time onward, painters and sculptors of the European tradition were able to free themselves from what

Feuchtmayer

This striking polychrome carving of Mary (1750) is full of the vitality and movement typical of Mannerist and Baroque sculpture.

**Masks from
New Guinea**

*These masks are
typical of those used
for initiation
ceremonies and other
rituals.*

had become for them an academic strait-jacket. Over the century, the view has gradually grown that any approach to artistic expression is valid. A danger is that originality may sometimes be valued over all other qualities.

It is important, however, to remember that the change of approach heralded by Picasso was not without precedent. Most of the labels attached to art movements, periods, and styles are unsatisfactory; but even if it is a gross over-simplification, broadly speaking we can apply the term "realism" to art forms which depict the world in as representational a way as possible, and "symbolism" to its opposite.

The evolution of European art has been likened to a pendulum swinging between the two. Its starting point was ancient Greece, whose classical art was the epitome of realism; the swing away from realism ended in Byzantium; the swing back from symbolism ended with the Renaissance in Italy; and the latest swing ended with Picasso in the early 20th century. The swings are not mechanical, but reflect the attitudes and thinking of the people of the time. The art of ancient Greece expressed the beliefs of a people whose gods were made in the image of physically perfect men and women; that of Byzantium echoed a religion more spiritual and mystical. The rediscovery of classical sources, which inspired the Renaissance, brought a return to realism in painting and sculpture.

The changing way in which we represent our world can be illustrated by comparing the cartoons of the 19th century, which required long captions, with those of today, which frequently need no explanation at all: a thought for those who can readily accept the distortions of a cartoon, but still reject a Picasso.

20TH-CENTURY CARVING

The carving trade remained largely untouched by changing artistic perceptions. A book on carving published in the 1930s barely acknowledged the styles of the early 20th century, such as Art Nouveau, but stuck firmly to the traditions of the 19th century. The book was reprinted in 1948 without a single change. Carvers did, occasionally, turn their hand to furniture and mirror frames in the latest style, but many continued to concentrate on reproducing the work of the past – and many still do. The best twentieth-century architecture, with its simple clean lines and its preference for forms that express its function, has virtually eliminated the demand for decorative ornamentation on buildings and furniture, so that commercial carving is largely confined to restoration and reproduction work. It would be self-conscious to try to drag traditional carving into the 20th century, and a rebirth of the fashion for carving in houses would almost certainly be precluded by expense alone. Other areas of carving, meanwhile, have evolved in keeping with modern ideas, from small-scale functional items to the wooden sculptures of Henry Moore and Barbara Hepworth.

Henry Moore
This large, tactile elm wood sculpture ("Reclining Figure," 1945–46) is reminiscent of the landscape, as well as the human figure. The grain of the wood emphasizes the forms.

Mauno Hartman
This mysterious wooden sculpture ("Peepuu," 1965) incorporates references to traditional Finnish objects.

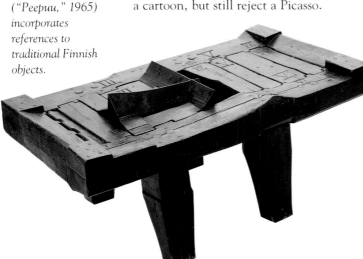

East African figures

Though it has a certain charm, the taller figure is a crudely carved tourist souvenir. The smaller figure, although for the tourist market, has been produced by a sensitive artist.

Zimbabwe mask
This mask is being carved with a knife instead of the more usual adze.

SOURCES OF INSPIRATION

In carving you are free to adopt any style you choose, but this very freedom can pose a problem when you are wondering where to begin and how to find your own means of expression. Unlike the carvers of the past, people today are constantly bombarded with images and visual influences from their own and other cultures. Modern means of travel have opened the whole world to tourists who look for and, of course, find souvenirs. Unfortunately, although a visitor can probably find a genuine African carving or a Welsh "love spoon" made by a sensitive artist, he or she more often accepts a travesty of indigenous art or craft made as cheaply as possible.

Even if we never travel, the latest art style is instantly brought to us by the media; and the art of most cultures, both historic and contemporary, can be seen in books, on film, in museums and galleries. Much of that art is powerful and impressive, and we cannot isolate ourselves from its influence, however bewildering. It is important to look at the work of accomplished artists and craftsmen and women, and try to understand their aspirations, but we should let their achievements enlarge our vision rather than trying to imitate them. Each of us has roots in a particular tradition, and if we can assimilate different ways of seeing, our work can be enriched without necessarily becoming eclectic.

There is great satisfaction to be gained from woodcarving, and this book is designed to help you discover and enjoy it.

Practical information and demonstrations introduce you to the techniques required for a variety of applications. Step-by-step instructions and photographs show you how to make particular projects, but also provide the principles you need to realize your own designs. A number of carvers have contributed projects, so that you can become familiar with a variety of different approaches.

John Roberts

This strikingly original sculpture, "Diana and Actaeon II," is carved in oak. The carver has assimilated elements of other cultures, but without imitating them.

Jonathan Mushlin

The design of this small carved box was conceived in much the same way as abstract sculpture.

MATERIALS & TECHNIQUES

DESIGN

The aim of the design process is to produce the best possible example of whatever you plan to carve. It should be satisfying to look at, pleasing to touch, and if it is a functional object, it should be well adapted to its purpose. Behind these considerations lie the individual perception and style that make the carving yours and nobody else's.

This individual dimension means that there can be no absolute rules for the design process. Carvers' priorities differ, and design requirements can vary in importance from one carving to another. However, carving needs a reasonably ordered approach, and there are guidelines to help you design effectively.

THE HUMAN DIMENSION

An important principle for me is to place the design within a human context. As human beings we see ourselves as the center of all things, not in a superficially arrogant sense, but simply because we experience the world through our bodies. Messages about everything we see, hear, touch, and smell are transmitted to, and interpreted by, our brains. The parts of the human body – arms and legs, hands and feet, fingers, thumbs, toes, and the rest – are all interrelated, and form the basis for comparisons between ourselves and every other object or inhabitant of the planet, animal or human. Before taking out a tape measure, people spontaneously use their hands to assess the size of an object in relation to themselves. Something designed in proportion to the human form is therefore likely to feel "right" – and that feeling can, of course, be deliberately subverted for artistic effect.

The significance of pleasing proportions dates back at least as far as Euclid (c. 300 B.C.), who probably first noticed the golden section, or golden mean. This is a particularly pleasing ratio between two dimensions, in which the lesser measure is to the greater as the greater is to the sum of both. Many paintings and buildings have been designed using the golden section – either deliberately or intuitively – to achieve a harmonious composition. Possibly the reason why we find it so congenial is that the same ratio of about 1.618:1 can be found between parts of the human body and the elements of many plants. Small wonder, perhaps, that Renaissance artists called it the Divine proportion.

The idea that all building should begin with the human body, because it contains the hidden secrets of measurement, attributed to the first-century Roman architect Vitruvius, was probably known to the architect Le Corbusier (1887–1965), whose harmonious scale, based on the proportions of the human figure, was set out in his book *Le Modulor* and realized in his buildings. The principle that applies to architecture can be extended to other things made by and for people. That is one reason why I have a great respect for traditional systems of measurement that are based on human beings and human activities. It seems to me that measures which relate to thumbs and feet and to the plowing of a furrow must have a greater affinity with human beings than a calculation involving part of a line from the North Pole to the equator.

FINDING YOUR OWN PERSPECTIVE

The furniture designer Thomas Chippendale (1718–79) lived in England, first in Yorkshire, then in London. He was an 18th-century man who saw the world through 18th-century eyes. However much we know about the 18th century, we cannot think as people did then. If we decide to carve a "Chippendale" mirror frame, we must acknowledge that this is a 20th-century person's version. Although our carving should have roots in tradition, it must also be informed by the world of today. We cannot ignore the visual stimuli, from the real world or from books and television, that have met our eyes since birth.

Looking at historical examples, one can see that design can be closely linked with fashion, and that fashion often looks dated. It is important to stand away from current fashion and try to isolate the essentials of design. The best design should come from seeing with our own eyes and interpreting in our own way, but without losing our respect for, and delight in, the work of other times.

INSPIRATION FROM NATURE

In sculpture there is a point between total realism and pure abstraction where optimum artistic interest lies. Happily, this point is different for each person. Referring to some heads by the Romanian sculptor Brancusi (1876–1957), Picasso is quoted as saying something like, "You can start with a head and gradually simplify the forms until you are left with an egg, or you can start with an egg, build on to it and end up with a head." Somewhere between the egg and the completely stated

Michael Lewis
This beautifully carved and gilded copy of a Chippendale mirror frame belies the often-heard statement that the carvers of today cannot match those of the past.

Thomas Chippendale the elder
This mahogany lyre-back library chair, made for Nostell Priory in 1768, shows the high quality of craftsmanship expected from the Chippendale workshops.

Grinling Gibbons

This beautiful composition shows why Grinling Gibbons has the reputation for being one of the most skillful carvers of all time.

and then be forgotten. What makes the work of carvers like Grinling Gibbons more interesting is its artistic imagination. There are some artists today who make their works by taking a mold from an arbitrarily selected spot somewhere on the Earth's surface. They then rebuild it using synthetic materials to make an exact copy. The technique is faultless, and the works are highly praised, but there is no intervention of the mind, which is, surely, an essential quality of art.

There are thousands of instances where nature is beautiful, or impressive, or terrifying – or all three simultaneously – but art lies at least partly in translating an individual experience of those manifestations. One famous example is "Snowstorm at Sea" by J.M.W. Turner (1775–1851). The artist and the designer must select and simplify, in order to create an illusion, or to fashion an object. The resulting object, whether two- or three-dimensional, has a presence of its own, which may be more or less reminiscent of the original experience; or it may recall more than one experience, as does, for instance, some of Henry Moore's work, which alludes to landscape and the human figure but is a naturalistic representation of neither.

head is the piece of sculpture which engages the imagination.

A carving may be technically perfect, with every hair or feather faithfully rendered, stir our admiration momentarily

Henry Moore

This magnificent sculpture in elm ("Reclining Figure," 1939), is reminiscent of eroded rocks and caves, as well as a human form. It epitomizes the sculptor's approach to carving.

CREATIVE DESIGN

How does all this affect the design of a wooden spoon? Well, more than you might at first suppose. If you want to carve a spoon, you can start with an existing spoon made in any material and imitate it. Or you can look at the situations in which your spoon will be used: the traditional bowl shape in the spoon will probably be needed; a curved side would be good for scraping around a bowl, but a right angle might be useful for getting into the corner of a saucepan, a gently sloping shoulder could be nicely cut out with a spokeshave. A rarely used serving spoon could have a more elaborate handle, but any spoon should be easy and pleasant to hold. Your spoon might not even be functional. You could design a spoon with a symbolic meaning, like the Welsh love spoon, or make your spoon the inspiration for a decorative pattern.

You draw your design and you carve it. It takes you a day and you could have bought a spoon for a few cents – but you have made one of your very own.

Joyce Hargreaves
This illustration of a "French Wyvern" from her book Hargreaves New Illustrated Bestiary *inspired the small carving "Vouivre Parisienne" (p. 61).*

STARTING POINTS

Nature is a rich area of inspiration, but ideas for carving can arrive from all kinds of unexpected sources if you keep an open mind and eye. Design requires visual thought, and that is helped by any kind of drawing – even doodling. Words can aid the process, especially those that stimulate images. Carry a sketchpad or notebook around with you and get into the habit of making thumbnail sketches of buildings, machines, people, and animals, or jotting down a brief detail of any image that impresses you. Photographs can be a valuable aid to memory, and an inspiration in themselves; and illustrations in books, magazines, and newspapers often stimulate ideas. Because we want to think three-dimensionally, sketch modeling in clay will also be useful.

Drawing is probably the greatest aid to design, not because you need drawing talent to carve wood, but because drawing can help you to understand the nature and structure of your subject. This does not mean that you must draw before carving. Drawings, photographs, and clay models all have a part to play in sorting out ideas, and for exploring forms.

GETTING STARTED

The practical part of designing may be no more than a sketch, it may be a sketch model, or it may entail carefully measured plans – sometimes all three. This preparatory work helps you to visualize the object and give you the necessary information to start carving, so you need only do what the piece seems to demand and what you yourself find useful.

Once you have chosen your subject, completed your research, and done some preliminary sketches, it is helpful to make a drawing or drawings, actual size if possible, or accurately to scale. For some objects a single view is sufficient, but the more three-dimensional the piece, the more necessary it is to draw a number of views to get an all-around image. For certain objects it is useful to design like an architect and draw plans and elevations, as shown here.

However much drawing you intend to do, you will need pencils, paper, a ruler, an eraser, and a drawing board. I cut a 16

plan

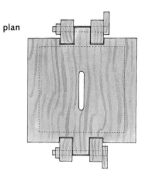

front elevation

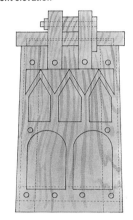

side elevation

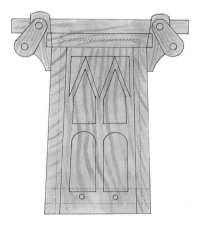

DESIGNING "IN THE ROUND"

When designing a three-dimensional carving, remember that its appearance constantly changes as you move around it. These eight views of a single figure are all different, and you could have a silhouette for every degree of the circle without duplication. Even if your design has a "most important viewpoint" – as, for example, in Bernini's *David* (1623) – you must still bear in mind all the other viewing angles in order to make a convincing piece.

Plans and elevations

You will find it helpful to draw up accurate plans and elevations for some of the projects in the book. The ones shown left are typical examples.

× 24 inch board from ½-inch Baltic birch plywood, allowing extra width to cut out a carrying handle, which is a boon on sketching trips. The paper can be held in place with clips or masking tape. If you plan to do precise technical drawing, such as orthographic projection, you will need more sophisticated equipment, and it makes sense to get the best you can afford.

DRAWING GRIDS

It may not always be practical to draw your design to size, or you may change your mind about its proportions. A photo-copier can help you enlarge or reduce it, but grids can be more useful. For instance, to increase an existing design to four times its present size, you could draw a grid of ¼-inch squares over the design and then make a grid of 1-inch squares on a clean sheet of paper for the target size, number-ing the squares in each case. This will enable you to enlarge the drawing accu-rately a square at a time as you copy it. The method is shown in more detail below.

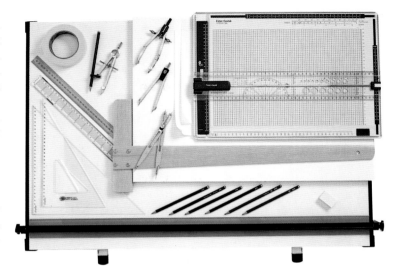

When you have an actual-size drawing, you can use identical grids to transfer the design to the wood. If the carving is com-plicated, it is a good idea to carry the lines down the sides of the wood and draw the grid on the back as well. This is because you will constantly be carving the pencil lines away, and even though

Drawing equipment

Shown here is a variety of instruments and equipment for drawing plans and elevations.

Scaling to size

Grids enable you to enlarge or reduce your drawing. Simply increase the size of the squares and then transfer the drawing square by square.

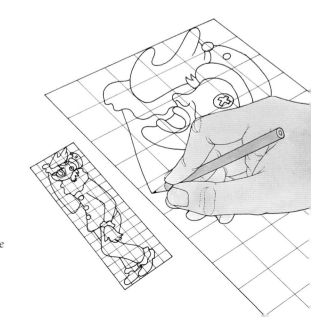

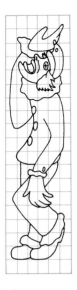

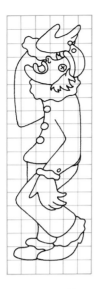

Changing proportions

The middle drawing can be made narrower or wider by changing the proportions of the grid and then transferring the drawing as before.

you will replace them, marks on the back will help in relocating points, especially when the piece is to be pierced.

Grids are also useful for altering the proportions of a design. For example, if you want your drawing to fit a narrower space, you can re-draw your grid on a clean sheet of paper, keeping the lines the same for the height but putting them closer together across the paper. You can then adapt the shapes in the squares to fit the grid of rectangles – giving a design that is thinner and looks taller. Alter it the other way to give a shorter, broader effect.

TEMPLATES

A template, or silhouette, of the design – sometimes with details cut through it like a stencil – can help when establishing the basic shapes on a block of wood, and later when part of the drawing has been carved away. Templates can be traced from your accurate drawings and cut from paper or poster board. Protect them with a few coats of shellac if they are likely to get damp. An excellent alternative is an orange template material used by stone-

masons, which is transparent and fairly rigid.

Templates can also be made from sketch models, as described on p. 22.

SKETCH MODELS

Some carvers are opposed to making a sketch model before carving, because, as they point out, modeling and carving are opposite processes: modeling involves addition and carving subtraction. Also, malleable substances like clay do not impose the disciplines of wood. The result, they argue, will be a copy of a clay model that will lack the qualities of direct carving. There is a lot to be said for these arguments, but it is not always easy for an ordinary mortal to visualize a three-dimensional object inside a piece of wood, and a sketch model can be an enormous help in at least two ways.

First, a rough sketch model is a way of thinking through a design, of trying out ideas and rejecting those which do not work. Second, an actual-size sketch model can be used to establish the depths and approximate shapes of the final form. Think in terms of woodcarving as you model, imagining how the shapes will carve, and leave your model as a rough sketch so that the final statement is made in the carving of the wood.

Modeling compound and clay are the most popular modeling materials because they can be used again and again. Modeling clay is suitable for small models and is relatively clean, though virtually impossible to remove if it is trodden into a carpet. Clay can be used for models of any size, but may need an internal support, such as a wire framework, for large models.

Modeling is done mainly with the fingers, but a few boxwood or steel tools are useful (see p. 22), and a cheesewire is good for cutting clay and for sliding under

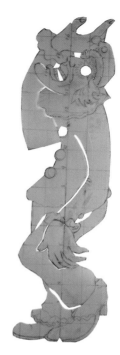

Templates

Templates can be made from paper, cardboard or specialist stone-mason's material as shown above.

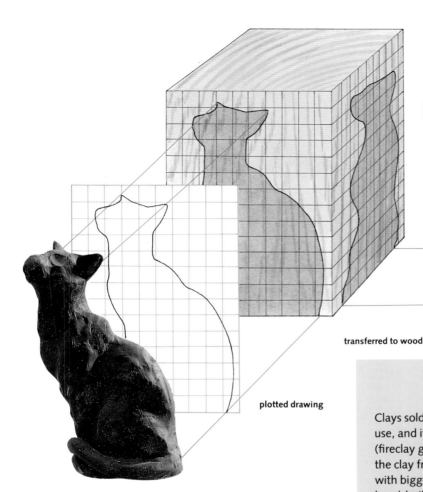

From sketch model to carving

First make a clay sketch model, then make an outline drawing. Draw a grid over your outline. Transfer both drawing and grid to the block of wood, freehand or using carbon paper.

profile cut from wood

transferred to wood

plotted drawing

sketch model

CLAY

Clays sold as "modeling clays" can be sticky and difficult to use, and it is worth buying potters' clay containing fine grog (fireclay ground to various mesh sizes). The grog helps to stop the clay from cracking as it dries and reduces shrinkage. Clay with bigger particles of grog incorporated can be used for large hand-built forms.

Clay will harden as it dries, so store it damp in a lidded plastic container. Cover it with a plastic sheet to exclude as much air as possible, and it will remain usable for a long time. When you have finished with a sketch model, or if your clay does become hard, leave it in the air until it is bone dry, then break it up and drop the bits into water, where they will quickly soften. Don't try to soften the clay until it has dried thoroughly, or it won't absorb water and you will be frustrated. Spread the soft clay on a porous surface, and when it has dried out enough, knead it to an even consistency. The clay can then be returned to the "damp container." To keep the clay damp while you are working on it, spray it from time to time with water. A small hand spray of the type used for plants is ideal for this. When you are not working on the model, wrap it in a sheet of plastic to stop it from drying out.

still soft models to remove them from the modeling board. It is always possible to improvise; for instance, bits of broken hacksaw blades are helpful for scraping away and for smoothing clay. Pencils, sticks, and old nail files all come in handy at times. For three-dimensional forms, it is worth having a modeling stand with a turntable, so that you can keep viewing the model from different angles; a small

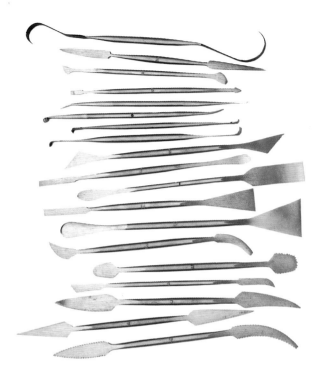

MAKING A TEMPLATE FROM A MODEL

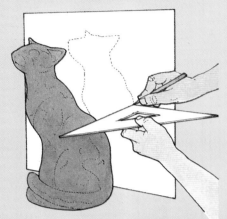

Templates are easy to trace from drawings, but making a template from a model involves the kind of projection used to make plans and elevations.

• Set up your model, and place your paper or poster board on a drawing board immediately behind it, parallel with the model's vertical axis. You can either work with the drawing board and model vertical or with both horizontal, in which case you may have to prop up the model so that its base is perpendicular to the drawing board.

• Select the silhouette you require: front and side views are usually chosen for three-dimensional models.

• Take a carpenter's square or try square and work around the model, making dots on the paper at points perpendicular to the same points on the model. The frequency of the dots depends upon the shape.

• Make sure that you have established the base line and the top and bottom points of the center line, if it is needed.

• Remove the model, connect the dots, and cut out the silhouette.

Modeling tools

Boxwood and steel tools are both useful for clay modeling. Buy a few initially and add to them as needed.

table stand is good enough for most jobs.

You can make your own modeling board from a piece of painted or varnished plywood or a plastic-coated surface. It is a good idea to draw grids on the board as well as the drawing and the carving, because if all three carry the same grid, it is quick and easy to relate them to one another. Draw the outline of the carving on the board, and build up the model with small pieces of clay.

To help you transfer measurements from your model to the wood, make a "bridge" which spans the model, on supports the same height as your piece of wood. Marking the bridge with lines equivalent to the grid will help to locate useful measuring points. When you start carving, use a depth gauge to measure down from your bridge to a point on the sketch model, then carve to an equivalent

point on your wood, but leave a little extra to be carved away later. Keep in mind that the model is only an aid.

MAKING A SKETCH MODEL

Although modeling is basically a process of building up forms, you can also remove material, using wire-ended tools or hacksaw blades. This makes modeling an ideal way of planning your approach to a carving and of visualizing and modifying your ideas three-dimensionally. Your aim is to arrive at an actual-size rough sketch which will show how the forms interact and dispose themselves, and will help you to gauge the depths to which you can carve. A good example is the mask for the Green Man (see p. 166).

1 Draw the outline on a piece of plastic-coated or painted board. Make a bridge the depth of the proposed carving to check the depth of your model.

2 Press clay onto the board within the outline, gradually building up the forms. You can use quite large pieces of clay to start with, but these should get smaller as you near the surface, so that you can press them easily into place with your thumbs and fingers.

3 One approach to this particular subject would be to model the face first and then to model the leaves on the face. Spray the model occasionally with water, and wrap it in plastic when not in use to keep it damp and malleable.

CHOOSING WOOD

Some woods are better for carving than others, but I believe it is worth trying any wood that is available. You may make a masterpiece, but if you don't, you will probably have learned from the exercise, and you might be able to use it to warm your workshop! I am sure that many good carvings have come from wood that was not thought suitable, and dare I say it, many bad carvings have emerged from perfect material.

There are strong arguments for not using woods which come from tropical rain forests and areas where erosion and flooding are being caused by indiscriminate cutting. Some endangered woods are now protected, and others are becoming increasingly rare.

A number of carvers and sculptors feel that there is a rightness about using wood that grows at least in their country or state, even if not on their own doorstep. Rather as a house built with local materials complements its surroundings, they consider that using local woods puts them in closer harmony with the environment and with traditional practices. Although it is a good idea to use local wood where practicable, your choice may be governed by considerations of availability and cost, and I would not exclude imported wood. If there is a wood on the shelf which is ideal for your carving, use it.

Bear in mind when choosing your wood the sort of carving you intend and the finish it will have. If your carving is to be elaborate and you plan to give it a natural finish, it is better to avoid wood with a pronounced grain pattern, or figure, which can make the carving difficult to see. In a simple, bold form, on the other hand, the grain of the wood can contribute to the final effect. If you intend to paint the carving on completion, these considerations will be unimportant.

The purpose of your carving may also have a significant part to play in your choice. If you are making a salad bowl, for example, you would avoid yew, which is poisonous, and you would probably not want other softwoods, such as cedar, which have a strong taste. Instead you could choose sycamore or poplar, or some other hardwood which you find attractive. For a purely decorative object, on the other hand, color and grain might be the governing factors for your choice.

BUYING WOOD

Many suppliers seem to stock blanks for turning and small ready-cut pieces for making stools, but no wood suitable for carving. Lumber yards are often happy to supply cut-offs (waste ends) and other fairly small pieces of wood, but it is worth checking before you visit. If you look them up in the Yellow Pages, you may also find a list of the woods they stock.

Antony Denning
"Portable Model"
carved in pear.

From enquiries at lumber yards, you may be able to track down a kiln, where wood is dried as part of the seasoning process and where you may be able to buy kiln samples relatively cheaply. These are good-sized pieces of wood taken out of the kiln to check on the progress of drying.

For small carvings you can sometimes pick up scrap wood from cabinetmakers' or woodworking shops. The so-called reclamation business, which stocks anything that can be salvaged from demolished buildings, can be a good source of well-seasoned wood, and lumber yards sometimes have similar items. This wood is liable to have a lot of nails in it, so it requires much care in handling and carving. Broken furniture in secondhand shops and furniture auction rooms can also provide worthwhile pieces. The seashore can be a source of driftwood, although you will need to rinse it thoroughly to remove salt. If you live in the country, you can often get pieces of fruitwood or other wood from people who have had to cut down an old tree. Landscape gardeners or tree surgeons might also be willing to let you have some wood. But if you use wood straight from the tree, you will have to season it.

There are numerous species of wood for carving, and the same type of tree can vary according to the conditions in which it grows. The list given here is therefore a general guide to some of the more widely available woods that carvers use. When choosing your wood, try to get it quarter sawn and without the center. Look for an even grain and no knots. Avoid sapwood – the wood between the inner bark and the heartwood – and pieces that have sunken parts.

SOME WOODS FOR CARVING

COMMON NAME	CHARACTERISTICS
POPLAR (*Liriodendron tulipifera*)	This is the wood of the tulip tree, sometimes confusingly called basswood in England. It seems to have, or have had, many names: saddletree, American whitewood, Virginian poplar, yellow poplar, yellowwood, canarywood, and canoe wood. It is fairly soft, close, and straight-grained, and has an even texture. The color varies quite a lot, from pale greenish-white to grayish-yellow; I have even seen some which were dark brown.
BOXWOOD (*Buxus sempervirens*)	The box shrub or tree does not grow large, so this wood comes in small sizes only. A hard, yellow wood, it is liked by experts for detailed work, but it does not carve easily.
CHESTNUT (*Castanea*)	Very similar to oak in appearance, but without the medullary rays. Less hard than oak, it is not difficult to carve. The wood is liable to have ring shakes (cracks that follow the annular rings), so check when you obtain it.
EBONY (*Diospyros*)	A dense dark or black wood, which tends to come in small sizes and is very hard to carve.

COMMON NAME	CHARACTERISTICS
HOLLY (*Ilex*)	A fine-grained, white or grayish-white wood, good for carving, and noted for its resemblance to ivory, alongside which it is sometimes used.
JELUTONG (*Dyera costulata*)	Straight-grained and fine-textured, it is known for being easily carved but uninteresting to look at, so it is usually painted. It is often used for rocking horses.
LIGNUM VITAE (*Guaiacum*)	A hard and dense wood, this is usually dark brown streaked with black, but it can have much lighter brown and greenish tinges. Difficult to carve, but can be highly polished.
BASSWOOD also known as LIME or LINDEN in England (*Tilia*)	One of the best woods to carve, with an even texture and close grain. Good for beginners and experts alike, this was the favorite wood of the marvelous German carvers of the 15th and 16th centuries, such as Tilman Riemenschneider and Veit Stoss, and of Grinling Gibbons in England. Its grain is scarcely apparent, and the original pale color can darken to a pleasant light brown with a pinkish tinge. It is particularly suitable for work containing detail and texture.
MAHOGANY (*Swietenia*)	This name covers a variety of tropical woods and the label is often extended to mahogany-like woods. Colors tend to be reddish-brown but can encompass shades from pale golden brown to deep red. Structure also varies: for example, Brazilian and Honduran mahogany can be good to carve, while African can have difficult grain.
OAK (*Quercus*)	A large family with European, Japanese, and American varieties. European oak is a pale fawn color which darkens to a pleasant brown; American oak can be pale or reddish; and Japanese oak has interesting subtleties of grain. Oak is hard though rewarding to carve, and is not recommended for work with fine detail. Avoid the sapwood, which is liked a lot by wood worms.
PEAR (*Pyrus communis*)	Pale yellowish-red to pinkish-brown, this is a good carving wood, close-grained and moderately hard.
PINE or YELLOW PINE (*Pinus strobus*)	A relatively soft yellowish wood, this carves well, but — as with all softwoods — the tools need to be very sharp and have longer bevels than those used for hardwoods.
SYCAMORE (*Acer pseudoplatanus*)	A white wood of the maple family, close-grained and hard, so quite difficult to carve. It is a popular choice for objects used for food.
WALNUT (*Juglans*)	Dense and dark brown, walnut carves well. Carvers tend to prefer walnut from Italy and American black walnut.

TOOLS AND EQUIPMENT

The traditional tools for woodcarving have changed little over the centuries, as early pictures and carvings show. A medieval bench end in the Provinzial Museum in Hanover portrays a monk using the round mallet still employed by woodcarvers and stonemasons, and he has some "fishtail" gouges in a rack on the wall. The bench end dates from *c.* 1285.

Before the 19th century, there was more likelihood of local variation because tools were made by individual craftsmen and may have been adapted to solve a particular problem. Tools were hammered out on a metal form known as a swage block, and if an itinerant toolmaker's block was worn, his fluters might have been $17/64$ inch instead of $1/4$ inch wide. It did not matter very much if the carvers who used them made the grooves, or flutes, on their moldings a fraction over a quarter of an inch wide. It is unlucky, though, for the modern carver working in the restoration field, who may need to have a tool specially made to reproduce a cut exactly.

Nineteenth-century industrialization brought greater standardization, but no loss of quality. For all the subsequent advances there may have been in metallurgy, it is still possible to find tools made over a hundred years ago that hold their edge better than some made today. The system of numbering the tools according to the degree of curvature of their end sections, regardless of width, combined with numbers to indicate their shapes in profile, aided standardization. Although there are still subtle differences between the tools and numbering systems of different toolmakers, they are fairly close, if not exact, matches.

People are often amazed at the number of tools required for woodcarving, especially compared with the relatively small range used for carving stone. One of my first instructors reckoned a trade carver might end up with as many as 200 tools; another thought 70 would be

Misericord

Most woodcarving is done standing, but this detail shows a medieval carver seated at his bench and is likely to reflect reality.

enough! In fact, as William Wheeler and Charles Hayward point out in their book *Practical Woodcarving and Gilding*, only about two dozen tools would be in constant use; others would be required occasionally, if urgently. A carver engaged in restoration, who has to match tool cuts with the originals, will need more than the carver doing new work.

It is therefore possible to do a great deal of woodcarving with relatively few tools, but each person's needs will vary according to their style and preferred subjects. Choice will also depend on the scale of your work, something you may not even know yourself when you start. If I am carving a figure 7 feet high, I shall have a different set of tools on the bench from those used to carve a piece 7 inches high. The best advice is to buy as few tools as possible to start with and gradually add to them as the need arises.

You may see sets of carving tools advertised in magazines or offered in craft shops. Some are good, but others are worthless, and even good sets will sometimes contain a tool that is seldom or never used. It is probably wise to avoid them and buy your tools singly. A basic list to get you started is shown below.

The tools that every woodcarver must have are chisels and gouges and a mallet. They come in a wide selection of shapes and sizes, and referring to the illustrations as you read will help you become familiar with them. Some makers supply chisels and gouges without handles (which are supplied separately). The suppliers will often attach the handles free, and it is worth taking advantage of that because attaching them can be tricky and if you don't get one straight, you have to attach another.

CHISELS AND GOUGES

Straight chisels and gouges A gouge is a chisel with a concave blade. Straight chisels and gouges are the strongest tools, used to do the bulk of the work. Most work with the mallet is done with them. Their sides are parallel nearly as far as the shoulder, and they are straight when looked at from the side.

Salmon bend, curved, long bent, double bent All these terms describe gouges with a long gentle curve. They are useful for carving bowls and hollow shapes where a straight gouge would start to dig in instead of flattening out as it neared the bottom. They are usually robust and will often be used with a mallet.

Bent, front bent, spoon/entering chisels and gouges The gouges do not get a lot of use unless you are carving a piece with fairly small but deep hollows. Bent chisels and corner chisels are also known as grounders or background tools, reflecting their usefulness in carving a flat background, for example, behind raised relief work, and for getting into awkward corners.

Back bent/back bent spoon gouges Seldom used, these gouges come in a very limited choice of sizes and shapes.

Dog leg chisel This is stepped instead of curved. It serves a similar purpose to the grounding chisel.

Fishtail/spade chisels and gouges The working part of these tools is triangular, which makes them particularly useful for detail carving. The terms used to be sub-

---

A BASIC TOOLKIT

Here are the tools to get you started. You can add to them when the need arises.

NUMBER/TYPE	SIZE
1 Straight chisel	½ in (13 mm)
2 Corner chisel/Skew chisel	½ in (13 mm)
3 Gouge (straight)	¾ in (20 mm)
8 Gouge (straight)	½ in (13 mm)
9 Gouge (straight)	⅝ in (16 mm)
11 Veiner (straight)	⅛ in (3 mm)
11 Veiner (straight)	3/16 in (5 mm)
39 Parting tool/V tool (straight) (about 60° angle)	¼ in (6 mm)
17 Gouge (salmon bend/long bent)	⅜ in (10 mm)
21 Chisel (bent)	¼ in (6 mm)
22 Corner chisel. Right (bent)	¼ in (6 mm)
23 Corner chisel. Left (bent)	¼ in (6 mm)
31 Gouge (bent)	⅜ in (10 mm)
65 Gouge (fishtail)	5/16 in (8 mm)
66 Gouge (fishtail)	⅜ in (10 mm)

(metric equivalents are not exact, and numbers may vary depending on the manufacturer)

Mallet Lignum vitae (if possible) 3 or 3½ inch, but try before you buy, and choose a weight that feels right.

Chisels and gouges

From left: 2 long fishtail gouges, straight gouge, salmon bend gouge, straight gouge, salmon bend parting tool (v), fishtail "v" tool, long fishtail chisel, straight chisel No. 1, skew chisel, back bent fishtail gouge, bent fishtail gouge, 2 bent corner chisels (English numbering).

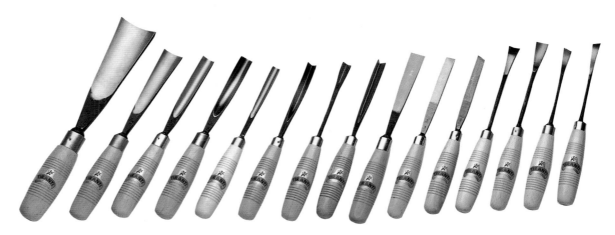

divided, so that the fishtail or spade tool had a small triangular end on a straight shank, the long-pod spade tool had a long slim triangle probably reaching about halfway up the shank, and the long-spade, or allongée, gouge or chisel was triangular as far as the shoulder. The tendency now seems to be to call them all fishtail. It is worth noting that some toolmakers make all their large tools – that is, ¾ inch (20 mm) wide or more – in the long-spade or full-length fishtail shape.

Sections Nearly all the tools described come in a variety of sectional shapes, and each section comes in a number of widths.

Carving tools

From top: No. 8 gouge, No. 9 gouge, salmon bend gouge, bent gouge, straight gouge, fishtail gouge, straight gouge, straight chisel, skew chisel, "v" tool, veiner (Swiss numbering).

Some catalogs list chisels or gouges of nine different sectional shapes, starting with ¹⁄₃₂ inch (1 mm), through about fifteen widths for each section up to 2 inches (50 mm) wide. Each section carries a number which applies to it, however narrow or wide it might be. For example, no. 1 is a straight chisel, and a straight chisel will be no. 1 whether it is ³⁄₁₆ inch (5 mm) or 1 inch (25 mm) wide.

Curved sections The curved section gouges are numbered from 3 to 11. No. 3 is the flattest, nearly a chisel; no. 11 is U-shaped. Nos. 10 and 11 are sometimes separated from the other gouges and called fluters (no. 10) and veiners (no. 11). The V-section gouges are called parting tools or V tools, and there is usually a choice of different angles. One which is about 60° is probably the best initially.

Macaronis, fluteronis, and backeronis Finally there are three less common shapes, which we shall not be using here: a macaroni, which has a channel-shaped section (three sides of a rectangle); a fluteroni, which is similar to a macaroni but with rounded corners; and a backeroni, which resembles a fluteroni with a low convex hump in the middle.

MALLETS

Though a large proportion of carving is done with two hands on the chisel or gouge – one hand pushing hard, the other restraining and guiding – there are times when a mallet is essential. For example, in the initial stages when roughing out, it is undoubtedly quicker to remove large amounts of waste with a gouge and mallet than with just your hands and a gouge. Carvers' mallets are round and are traditionally made of beech or lignum vitae (p. 26). There are now very good plastic mallets, but they tend to be too big for any but large-scale work. Lignum vitae is excellent because its density allows the mallet to be smaller than one made of beech. It is important to choose a mallet that feels comfortable in use, so handle it before you buy it.

One of my favorite tools is the so-called dummy mallet which has a malleable iron

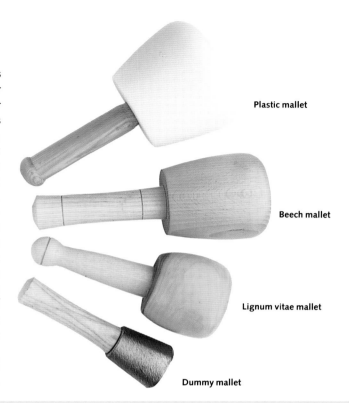

Plastic mallet

Beech mallet

Lignum vitae mallet

Dummy mallet

A TOOL ROLL

Once you have got really sharp tools, it is worth protecting the edges as much as possible by storing them in a tool roll. This pattern is designed for 20 chisels and gouges. It is easy to increase or decrease the size, but I don't think I would go above 30 in one roll because it would become awkward to handle. Traditionally tool rolls were made of green baize, but burlap or canvas will do very well. Pockets for the tool handles are staggered so that the edge of a tool on one side lies between two handles of the tools opposite. The side flaps not only protect the edges, but stop tools from sliding out. Two straps and the end flap keep it all together when it is rolled up.

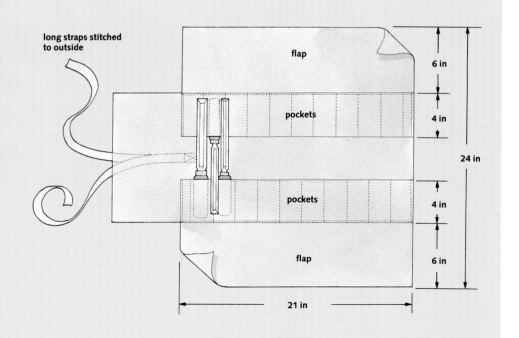

long straps stitched to outside

flap

6 in

pockets

4 in

24 in

pockets

4 in

flap

6 in

21 in

or lead head; it nestles in the hand and is very useful for making controlled cuts with gentle tapping, as in letter cutting or following around a curve.

ADDITIONAL TOOLS

A number of tools which are used by carpenters and cabinetmakers will be indispensable, and others can be a great boon. You will need saws, and a ruler, tape measure, square, plane, scrapers, and a spokeshave. Other useful tools include rasps and shaver tools, marking gauges, dividers or calipers, hand drills and braces with bits. Rasps and shaver tools are more likely to be used on large sculpture than on carvings. Rifflers, which are small,

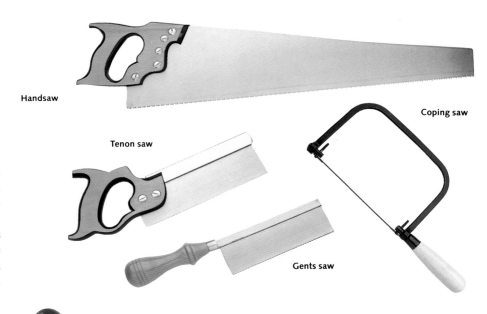

Handsaw

Coping saw

Tenon saw

Gents saw

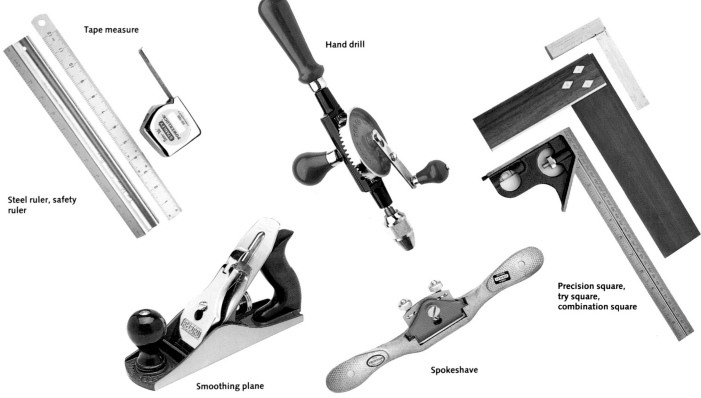

Tape measure

Hand drill

Steel ruler, safety ruler

Precision square, try square, combination square

Smoothing plane

Spokeshave

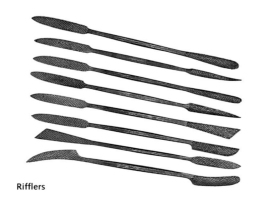

Rifflers

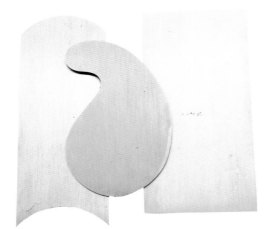

Cabinet scrapers

shaped rasps, occasionally help in cleaning up the underside of a pierced part, which is rather like a bridge but beyond the reach of even a back bent gouge.

POWER TOOLS

In this book we shall be concentrating on hand tools, but power tools will sometimes be mentioned. There are undoubtedly occasions when a power tool makes a job quicker and easier – cutting rabbets in the backs of frames, for example. If you have the tool and the knowledge to use it, you will probably see for yourself where it would make sense to use it. Remember that power tools tend to make a lot of dust, and some are noisy, so you cannot really use them in a kitchen or dining room. Some of the most useful tools are illustrated here, but there is a huge choice to tempt you, and it is better to wait until you are sure which ones you need.

Bandsaw

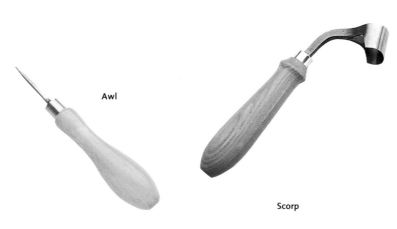

Awl

Scorp

Electric drill and chuck key

Jigsaw

MAKING A SCRATCH STOCK

To make a length of molding like that on the mirror frame in project 9, you can create your own tool, known as a scratch stock, which consists of a holder and a shaped blade. The dimensions of the stock will depend upon the profile of the molding, but one or two stocks will serve most purposes.

1 Take a regular-shaped piece of hardwood, such as beech, about 1 inch thick. Remove a right-angled portion which is both deeper and longer than the proposed blade. Drill a number of holes right through to take slightly dome-headed slotted bolts. On one side draw around the correctly positioned nuts and countersink suitably shaped holes into the wood deep enough to enclose the nuts. With

the bolts removed, draw the center line all around the wood and saw it in half. Bolt the two halves together. Next make a thin cardboard template of the molding profile. Use a hacksaw to cut a rectangular blank, slightly larger than the profile, from, for instance, an old wood-saw blade.

2 Draw around the template, and holding the blank in a metal vice, file away the reverse of the molding. The edge should be square. Burrs can be removed by rubbing on an oil stone, and the blade can be sharpened using slipstones or smooth files.

3 Loosen the bolts, fit the blade in the stock, and re-tighten. If the blade gets in the way of a bolt, it is usually satisfactory to leave one bolt out. Mark the profile on the ends of the wood and draw lines to indicate the limits of the waste which can be taken off the top and edge. Plane away as much waste wood as you can, continuing with a gouge if it is appropriate to the design.

4 Use the scratch stock to finish the molding. Grip it firmly so that the stock sits against the edge of the molding and work the blade back and forth along the length. Scrape only a little bit away at each stroke.

5 The finished profile.

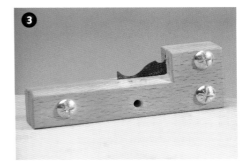

SHARPENING YOUR TOOLS

The chisels and gouges used for carving must be very sharp. Some toolmakers supply their tools ready to use, so that, to begin with, they only need occasional stropping on dressed leather. Others sell the tools ground (partly sharpened on a grindstone), but the carver has to hone, or fine-sharpen, them before use.

Unlike chisels used for other forms of woodwork, the carving chisel has a slight angle, or bevel, on the upper side of the cutting edge as well as the larger bevel on the underside, and it is sharpened on both sides. Similarly, carvers' gouges normally have a bevel on the inside as well as the predominant bevel on the outside. This enables the carver to use the tool either way up without its digging in, reduces friction, and makes cutting easier.

Sharpening is done on an abrasive stone, keeping the tool at a constant angle and maintaining an even pressure on the cutting edge. The method will vary slightly according to the tool you are sharpening. Sharpening is followed by polishing on a leather strop, which also removes the fine "wire" that remains from the sharpening. Occasional stropping as the carving proceeds will help to keep the edge sharp and delay the inevitable moment when the tool will have to be resharpened. Where an edge is damaged, it may be necessary to re-grind on a grindstone. The grind-stone should be relatively slow and water-cooled to preserve the temper of the steel. If there is no grindstone available, it is often possible to carry out the operation on a coarse oilstone, following which the tool should be sharpened on a fine stone and stropped.

STONES FOR SHARPENING

Stones for sharpening can be either oil-stones or waterstones, and it is probably better to stick to one type. Both come in a range of grades from coarse to fine, and both are equally good. Oilstones have to be lubricated with thin oil, oil, and kero-sene, or a patent preparation; they are harder than waterstones and last longer.

Grindstone

This slow, water-cooled grindstone is powered by an electric motor and has a leather-covered honing wheel. The exchangable jigs help to keep the angle of grinding constant. Other good models have a horizontal grinding wheel.

Stones
Oilstones, slipstones, and Japanese water stone (top right).

SHARPENING CHISELS AND GOUGES

Tools are sharpened by grinding, honing, and stropping. You can often buy them ready-ground or even ready for use, but they will need re-sharpening at times and should be stropped to keep them sharp during carving.

1 To sharpen a chisel, keep it at a constant angle while pushing it back and forth on a flat, lubricated oilstone. (If you alter the angle, the cutting edge will become slightly rounded and therefore inefficient.)

2 Carry out the finer sharpening, or honing, with the same movement but on a hard, smooth stone, such as an Arkansas, or a soft, fine-grit waterstone. Sharpen both sides of the cutting edge.

3 Strop the chisel by drawing it firmly backward on a piece of dressed leather.

Natural oilstones, such as Arkansas, are expensive but should last a lifetime.

If you choose oilstones, I suggest a combination stone which has a coarse or a medium grit on one side and a fine grit on the other. Sharpening with these could be followed by use of a translucent white Arkansas stone, and then a black Arkansas, which is the finest. The inner bevels of the gouges are honed with small stones known as slips which as nearly as possible match the shape of the gouge, so you will also need a selection of these.

If you are buying waterstones, choose a coarse-grade stone – say, 800 grit – and a finishing stone of 6000 grit, and again an assortment of slips to fit as many shapes and sizes of gouge as possible.

After honing, the tool is stropped on soft leather, which has been dressed with a patent dressing or with crocus powder and tallow. Jewelers' rouge, which largely consists of crocus powder, can be used instead. Russian tallow is usually recommended, but may not be easy to obtain. The leather can be stuck to a flat piece of wood for stropping chisels, and folded around pieces of dowel or shaped wood for treating the inner bevels of gouges. Keep strops covered when not in use to prevent dust and grit from spoiling them.

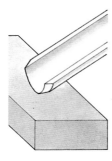

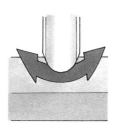

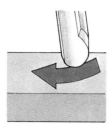

When sharpening gouges, rock the tool back and forth as you move across the stone. This will sharpen the entire bevel evenly. Take care not to remove the corners.

④ Gouges have to be sharpened with a lateral rocking movement. Hold the gouge so that it faces across the stone near the far edge. As you move it back and forth along the stone, rock it so that every part of the curve is sharpened evenly. Be careful not to round off the corners. The blade should be square in silhouette – neither concave nor convex unless it is sharpened for a specific purpose.

⑤ Sharpen the inner bevel with an appropriately shaped slip stone, rocking it slightly to curve the bevel. Use a finger and thumb to prevent the slip stone from sliding off at the corners.

⑥ Strop the outer bevel with the same movement as for honing. Strop the inside bevel with folded leather or glue the leather to a piece of wood shaped like the slip stone. Both chisels and gouges have straight bevels viewed from the side, but the heels are slightly rounded for smoother cutting.

⑦ Sharpen parting tools as if they were two chisels. Normally they do not have an inner bevel, but are cleaned up with a triangular slip stone. A small hooked point is often left at the bottom of the V which you should rub off with a slip stone, creating a slightly rounded V. A piece of string or a leather bootlace, dressed with strop dressing, is useful for stropping the inside of fine gouges and V tools.

⑧ A further refinement favored by some carvers is to grind the edges of gouges and chisels on one or both sides of the bevel. If an edge is damaged, or gets out of shape, use a grindstone to straighten it and to replace the bevel. Make sure that the grindstone is water-cooled or the temper will be taken out of the steel.

Gouges

Incorrect sharpening will remove the corners (top); they should remain sharp (center). However, you can remove one side if you need to enter an acute corner (bottom).

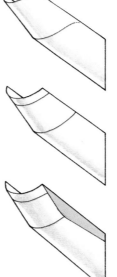

Inner bevel

The inner bevel is sharpened with a slipstone and polished with a folded leather strop.

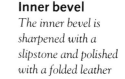

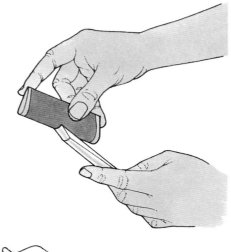

Chisels

If you remove the square corners on one side of a chisel (top) it will allow you to work in an acute corner.

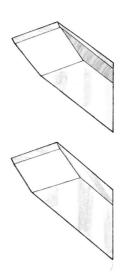

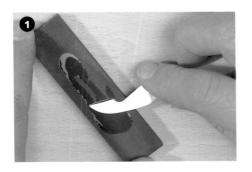

Sharpening chip carving knives

1 Use a small fine silicon carbide stone with thin oil to hone a knife blade. Hold a chip knife at a 10° angle and a stab knife at a 30° angle and make forward and backward movements.

2 Strop the knife with leather dressed with an abrasive compound such as jeweler's rouge or crocus powder – as often as a pool player chalks a cue!

SHARPENING SCRAPERS

Scrapers remove fine shavings and are good for jobs such as smoothing crossed grain. They are sharpened by turning a burr on both sides of their long edges.

1 File the long edges flat and square and remove any remaining "wire."

2 and **3** Grind the long sides and edges smooth on a flat oilstone and hone, in the same way, to a fine finish on a stone such as an Arkansas.

4 Put a burr on the four long edges using a burnisher: a smooth, hardened steel rod about ⅜ inch in diameter and 5 inches long, set in a wooden handle. Press or clamp the blade onto the bench, jutting over the edge by about ³⁄₁₆ inch. Then rub the scraper edge, using as much pressure as you can. Start at the corner nearest to you with the burnisher handle downward, so that the rod leans over the blade at between 80° and 85°. Rub away from yourself and slightly downward. A few strokes should be sufficient for each edge. Curved scrapers are best held in a vise for filing and clamped for burnishing.

5 Use the scraper at an angle of between 60° and 80°. You can push it away from you, or draw it toward you, as shown here.

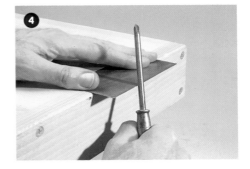

THE WORKSHOP

It is worth giving some thought to where you are going to work. You need a space where you can make a mess without its mattering too much. You need good light, and daylight is by far the best.

Fluorescent lighting is suitable as background illumination, but it should be augmented by at least one strong lamp which can be directed, so that you can see shadows cast by unevennesses which do not show up in a diffused light. It can be quite a shock to take a piece into the daylight after working under fluorescent lighting and to see what you have missed.

A WORKBENCH

A solid bench or working surface is desirable. Most carvers work standing up, because it is often easier to exert the right force from a standing position, but it is certainly possible to sit. Whether you sit or stand, however, it is important to have your work surface at a comfortable height. It is not good to have to hold your arms up to get at the work, nor to stoop over it too much. To avoid getting tired quickly, you must be able to use your hands in as relaxed a posture as possible. If you are sitting, table height should be suitable. For carvers who prefer to stand, I have seen specific heights suggested – 37¾ inches and 48 inches, for example – but these pre-suppose that people are the same. My workbench is 39½ inches high, and I would find 48 inches very un-comfortable. The best way to find a con-venient height for your bench is to stand with your upper arms straight down by

WORKSHOP SAFETY

As with most occupations, carving can be dangerous, and it is essential to take a few sensible precautions to prevent possible accidents. If you bear in mind that to carve effectively you need very sharp tools, you will probably treat them with respect. What may be less obvious is that the dust from sawing and sanding, particularly with power tools, can be hazardous and even poisonous. For instance, all the parts of yew are reported to be poisonous, although yew is a desirable wood for sculpture and can be safely carved. Always bear the following points in mind.

- Have a first aid kit in the workshop.
- Your working surface must be firm.
- Make sure the piece you are carving is securely held by a device. You need both hands for carving.
- Always test the sharpness of your tools on a scrap piece of wood, never with your fingers.
- Work in a good light.
- Have the floor around you reasonably clear and clean. There should be nothing to trip or slip on.
- Wear a mask and eyeshields when using power tools, and ear defenders with the noisier ones.
- Power tools come with safety instructions, and it is important to read and follow them to the letter.
- If you are making a lot of dust, try to work outside. If you have to be inside, use an exhaust fan. Always use a dust mask.
- Don't blow sawdust out of a cavity unless you are wearing eyeshields.
- Don't neglect splinters – some people react badly to them, particularly if they come from some exotic hardwoods. Check with your doctor if you think a cut or splinter is becoming infected.
- Don't carve toward yourself.
- Don't carve when you are tired.
- Store your tools safely and replace them carefully as you work. If they roll off a cluttered worktop, they can damage themselves and you.
- Clear away shavings to reduce fire risk.

your sides and your forearms and hands straight out in front, that is, perpendicular to your upper arms: the bench top should come about an inch under your forearms.

Your working surface should be well anchored, especially if you are using a mallet, but the top need not be very big: mine is 20 by 42 by 2 inches thick.

HOLDING THE WORK

Both hands are needed for carving, so the piece being carved must be held securely. The holding device will vary according to the type of work. A strip of molding, for instance, might be held down fairly crudely with nails at each end. A fretted piece that is rather fragile can be glued to a larger board with two or three layers of newspaper in between to make removal easy when the carving is finished. The board can then be held with one or two C-clamps. This method is also useful for securing a relief carving where you need continuous access to all parts of the piece. When there is no danger of tools striking them, you can use screws to secure backing board to it. A carver who is making a series of pieces the same size might devise a jig to hold them.

Sometimes it is possible to hold the work itself with C-clamps or with a bench holdfast (see p. 40). Woodworkers' vises are also suitable, especially the kind known as carvers' vises. When placing your work directly in a clamp or vise, you may have to pad it first to prevent denting or strain – pieces of cork, leather, or soft wood can provide good protection.

An ingenious gadget is the "universal work positioner," consisting of a circular plate to which a piece of work can be fixed. The plate can then be swivelled and tilted to whatever position is required and locked there until the carver wants to change it. This makes it easy to keep

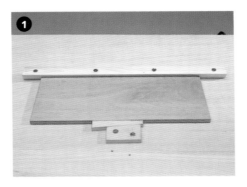

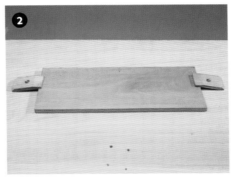

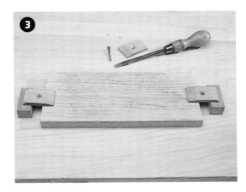

viewing the carving from different angles. In contrast, one of the simplest effective ways of holding a piece is the cobblers' strap. A length of webbing, a leather strap, or plaited sisal is firmly attached on the far side of the bench, taken over the work, and kept tightly in place by the carver's foot in a stirrup at the strap's end. This could literally be a stirrup, and the length of the strap could be adjusted at that end, or you could make a permanent loop and adjust the length of the strap from the fixed end. It only takes seconds to move the piece to a new position.

Note: Many of the demonstration photographs had to be taken using a bench lower than the recommended height, but prolonged use of a low bench would be tiring and could cause backache.

IMPROVISED DEVICES

In addition to the devices you can buy to hold your work, there are others that you can adapt or improvise, including those shown here. Additional solutions are bound to suggest themselves as you go along. You should always pad work which might otherwise be dented when clamped, for instance, and for that you could use a pencil eraser or a piece of cardboard. Alternatively, if you have cut a shape with a coping, jig, or band saw, the scraps provide ideal padding.

1 and **2** Methods for holding thin panels.

3 A modification for thicker panels. In **2** and **3**, the nearer the screws are to the work, the stronger the hold.

4 The V block to hold, for example, a cylindrical shape. Note the hardwood stop set into the 90° V groove. This allows you to plane the shape after removing the cramp and holding the block in a vise.

5 and **6** Alternative ways of holding

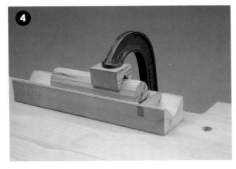

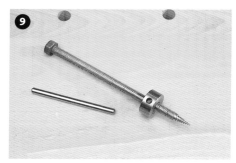

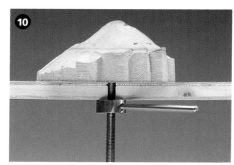

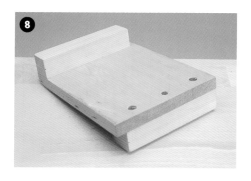

balls for drilling. For **5**, first make a hole the same diameter as the sphere and about three-quarters of its depth. Then saw the block in half down its length. If this does not give a tight enough fit, plane the saw-cut faces to allow more pressure to be applied in the vise.

7 Delicate work glued to a board with posterboard or paper in between. The board can then be held with clamps. More robust pieces can be screwed to a board from behind. The base board can be thicker, allowing it to be held in a vise.

8 A bench hook.

9 A carvers' bench screw (German pattern).

10 Cutaway view of a carvers' bench screw passing through the work surface and screwed into the base or back of the carving, with the nut tightened on the underside.

11 A bar clamp used to hold a spindle while a double spiral is being carved. Some 1 × 2 inch blocks are placed on each end of the clamp beam.

12 A scrap piece of wood can be screwed or clamped to the bench to stop the work from rotating during carving.

13 A bench holdfast in use.

HOLDING TOOLS

Before you start to carve, try your tools on scrap wood, with a mallet where appropriate, as well as without. The illustrations below show some general principles, but as you go through the projects, look carefully at all the photographs where tools are used. Much carving consists of scooping cuts where you enter the tool at a fairly steep angle, which allows it to bite, and then swinging the handle down through a curve as you strike a succession of blows with a mallet.

❶ Making an almost vertical stabbing cut.

❷ A fairly steep angled cut suitable for entering.

❸ Nearing the end of a scooping movement. The same technique applies when using two hands.

❹ Using the right hand to push hard and the left to control and restrain the gouge. Aim to be able to swap hands and go back in the opposite direction, pushing with the left and controlling with the right hand.

TRIAL BLANKS

Having spent time seeing what your tools will do, it is a good idea to develop your control by carving simple objects, such as these blanks. You can vary the design and shape, and you could turn the results into an attractive box or table lamp. The first attempts can always become hot plates for hot dishes if nothing else. When designing the blanks, your main concern is to match the cuts to the gouges and V tools which you possess, and then arrange the cuts to make a pattern.

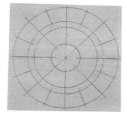
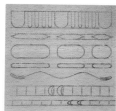

Four 5-inch square beechwood blanks with outline patterns drawn on them in pencil.

Method

The illustrations below left show four 5-inch square beech blanks with their outline drawings. There is no set order for making the cuts, but it is sensible to do all the carving you can with one tool before changing to another. Note that with all stabbing cuts in a hard wood like beech, it is better to stab part of the way, remove a chip, and then stab again. It is easier on the wood, the tool – and you.

1 Carve the V grooves across the grain before those with the grain. Here a No. 39 V tool ¼ in (6.5 mm) is being used. Do not try to go to the full depth immediately, but make several cuts, gradually getting deeper. The dividing ridge between the two V grooves is delicate.

2 and **3** Before cutting into the corner gently stab (at the same angle as the V) the corners where the grooves will meet. Using a mallet gently gives more control than pushing.

4 Cut the small notches towards the line with a 5/16 in (8 mm) No. 8 or 9 gouge.

5 Gently tap your V tool along the line to cut the groove. The innermost groove is curved in section and is carved with a ⅛ in or 3/16 in (3 mm or 5 mm) No. 11 gouge. The short grooves of different widths are made by stabbing vertically with a chisel or gouge, followed by going in fairly steeply but immediately scooping and then carving horizontally toward the stabbed cut, from the other end.

6 Working on the repeat cuts of the blank illustrated top right. Stab straight down with a 3/16 in (5 mm) No. 11 gouge.

7 Using the same gouge, remove the chip with one cut. The wider cuts in the next row are made in the same way, but with a ½ in (13 mm) No. 7 or 8 gouge.

8 A bent tool is being used here but is not essential. A ⅛ in (3 mm) No. 10 or 11 gouge would be suitable. Make the groove in stages, removing a small amount

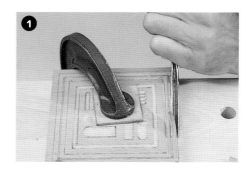

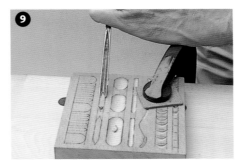

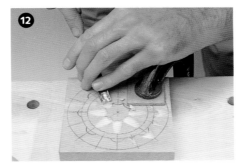

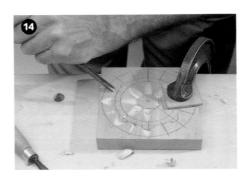

in the first cut, following the wavy line.

9 Come in from each end to make the double-ended V cuts, using the ¼-in (6.5 mm) No. 39 V tool. The larger shallow shapes can be made with a ⅝ in (16 mm) No. 8 or 9 gouge. Go in fairly steeply at the ends and quickly curve the handle down so that your gouge is at a very shallow angle. Work from both ends and aim to keep the bottom horizontal.

10 Carve the narrower grooves in the same way using a ³⁄₁₆ in (5 mm) No. 11 gouge. The side grooves, which end in a straight line, should have their straight ends made with a stabbing cut from a chisel of the appropriate width. Be careful here, because a succession of stabbing cuts along a straight line can cause the wood to split.

11 Some of the grooves in the rosette are carved diagonally across the grain. They cannot be carved straight down the axis, or the wood will tear. Instead you must work your gouge either with or across the grain, according to which side of the groove you are carving.

12 Use several small slicing cuts. Carve the tapering grooves to the center with a ½ in (13 mm) No. 7 or 8 gouge. Make steeply sloping cuts round the central "boss," then carve a gently sloping cut in toward it to give the taper.

13 Create the outer ring in the same way, but stab the inner cut more vertically. Tip the gouge one way and then the other at the end of the cut to remove the last little sections on each side.

14 Use a ¼ in (6.5 mm) V tool for the alternate cuts of the outer ring. The stab cut at the inner end is made with a ¼ in (6.5 mm) chisel.

15 The pattern on the blank (bottom right) is made in the same way. You can use a ½ in (13 mm) No. 7 or 8 gouge for the tapered grooves and a ³⁄₁₆ in (5 mm) No. 11 gouge for the continuous square "spiral."

CARVING PANELS
IN RELIEF

The method for carving panels in relief consists of three basic procedures – grounding, setting, and shaping – done in eight steps whose key aspects are illustrated here.

1 Draw the design on the wood. This design is set against a plain flat background, so use your marking gauge to indicate the depth of the background all the way around the edge.

2 Grounding, or cutting away the background, is done in several stages. Begin with the largest No. 8 or 9 gouge appropriate to the size of your panel. Keep well outside the line and carve to within about 1/16 in (2 mm) of the background level.

3 Setting is the process of cutting vertically around the line of the design. First carve a groove around the main outline with a small No. 9 or 11 gouge. Stay about 1/16 inch outside the line and do not bother with precise detail.

4 Then stab vertically down to just above the background level, all around and marginally outside the main outline. Use a fairly flat gouge, such as a No. 5, and continue to ignore the finer detail.

5 Ground into the line you have just set

in, using the same gouge. Then set in again, this time using different gouges to follow the lines as exactly as possible. Keep above the background level.

6 You are now ready for the third stage of grounding in; use a wide, fairly flat gouge to remove the wood to background level. You can check with a straightedge to see how flat it is.

7 Shaping means roughly carving the general shapes, which is done with bold, sweeping cuts. Re-draw any lines you need after cutting them away. You will now have reached the point illustrated below.

8 To complete the panel, carve and trim the final shapes (a last setting in), undercut, and finish the background (the final grounding).

The panel with all the shapes roughly carved in.

MAKING FRAMES: CUTTING A RABBET

A rabbet is the recess in the back of a frame and is best made before the corner joints.

(1) Cut the four sides for the frame a little longer than the final dimensions. Plane the best faces flat and square to each other for the fronts and sides. Mark these clearly where the planes meet and make all your measurements from these levels, known as reference edges.

(2) Plane the inside edge of each side of the frame square with the front and parallel with the reference edge. Measure down from the front to the edge of the rabbet and mark it along the length. On the back, pencil in the line showing the width of the rabbet.

(3) Hold one side in a vise and remove the waste wood by chiseling or planing the corner off and using a gouge to take out as much of the remainder as possible. Finally clean up with a sharp carpenters' chisel.

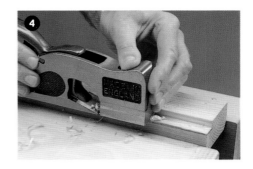

❹ A rabbet plane makes the job quicker, but do it in several stages. First take out about half the width to nearly the full depth. Next come in from the side to the full width, and third, finish it to its full depth.

❺ You could also use a plow plane. Do this in two stages, first cutting to the full depth along the line of the full width, and then coming in from the side. Some crafters prefer not to make the second cut at the full depth, but leave a little to be cleaned up with a chisel.

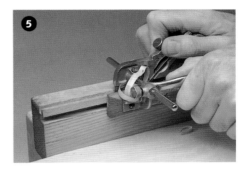

(6) This rabbet runs the full length. If it is not to do so, it must be made with chisels and gouges, at least in the corners where rabbet planes and plow planes cannot reach.

MAKING FRAMES: USING A LAP JOINT

The lap joint makes a strong corner.

(1) Using a try square against the prepared reference faces, mark the center lines lightly with a pencil. Working from the center lines, measure and mark half the length of the inside of the frame pieces. Draw a line all around at each end.

(2) In the mirror frame project, the top and bottom pieces have the backs cut away and the fronts of the side pieces are treated in the same way. Arrange the four pieces with the top and bottom lying across the sides in the positions they will occupy. Number each joint and scribble on the portions to be removed.

(3) Place your craft knife on the line, slide the try square up to it, and draw across with the knife; do the same at each end of all four pieces. Use a marking gauge from the reference faces to mark a line halfway across the thickness of the wood on the sides and ends of the laps.

(4) Shade clearly all the parts to be removed. Hold the wood on a bench hook to make saw cuts across the grain. Saw on the waste side of the line down to the gauge marks on the sides.

(5) Hold the frame side at an angle in a vise and saw diagonally from the inner to the outer corner, again on the waste side of the line. Angle the wood the opposite way and saw diagonally down to the inner corner on the other side.

(6) Reposition the frame side upright and saw through the remaining triangle.

❼ Secure the frame side with a C-clamp or a vise to clean up the joint with a chisel.

❽ Assemble the frame to check it. Then glue, clamping each joint when it is square.

DEALING WITH DEFECTS

However careful you are, you may occasionally cut too deeply or break a piece off your carving. Defects can also be inherent in your material, or you may inherit them when repairing or restoring. The solution will depend on the carving, its purpose, and intended final finish.

When you are faced with a defect in the wood, it is worth stopping to think about it. If the piece is a commission, that might influence your decision – or the client might. If it is a sculpture or decorative object, your attitude could be different from your thoughts about the lovely salad bowl you were carving. Ask yourself: Is it possible to ignore the defect? It might be less obvious left alone than it would be if remedied. Is it possible to re-design or adapt the piece so that the defect can be carved away? Might it be better to start again? For instance, the salad bowl could become a fruit bowl, where the defect probably would not matter. Then you could put it down to experience and begin another salad bowl.

When the defect has to be repaired, the finish becomes important. If the object is to be painted, you can glue, or "piece in," some wood, or use a synthetic resin filler, and the paint will disguise the repair. For a "natural" finish, you will have to piece in matching wood of the same sort.

It does occasionally happen that you find a dead knot or a crack, known as a shake, in the course of carving a piece of wood which had appeared to be perfectly sound. This happened to me when I was carving a coat of arms in three-inch bass-wood. I came across a dead knot (of which there had been no sign on the surface of the wood) that ran right across the motto scroll and part of a heraldic dolphin for about 5 inches. The only satisfactory answer was to cut it out and piece in a strip about 1 × 1 × 5 inches. Even though the work was to be painted and gilded, it would have been difficult to use a filler because much had still to be carved. I have come across shakes or cracks in bass-wood blown down in a gale – probably caused by the violent fall of the tree. In this case the size of the cracks and the intended finish made it possible to use an epoxy resin filler. If a shake has to be filled with wood for a natural finish, tap in a lightly glued triangular strip, being careful not to leave any traces of glue, which could reject a stain. When the glue has set, shave the strip back to the surface of the carving. If the defect is very narrow, you can fill it with one of the specially formulated colored waxes used by cabinetmakers and restorers.

Pieces broken off during carving can usually be glued back quite easily. Carvers in the past are reputed to have broken pieces off deliberately to gain access to awkward areas of carving; so before you replace the piece, check whether you can take advantage of the accident in this way. Be careful to keep the broken edges as they were when they parted company, then they will glue back together more easily. Cutting too deeply is more difficult to remedy. Usually the only solution is to carve all around the cut until it appears to have been what you intended from the start. If you go through the bottom of a bowl (not unprecedented!), you can probably do little more than count up to ten and recycle the wood. If you cannot even get some wooden spoons out of it, you may have to let the wood-burning stove do the recycling while you begin the next project.

SOME TYPICAL REPAIRS

Splitting caused by drying out

Wood dries out or absorbs moisture as it strives to maintain a balance with the surrounding humidity, which is why seasoning is important. Seasoning takes time, but there is pressure to meet the requirements of industry, so it can be difficult to buy the large sections of wood needed for sculpture in a stable enough condition. The wood may still contain too much moisture, and sudden drying can cause it to split.

1 The early stages of a carved head. As you carve into a block, you increase the surface area through which moisture is lost, and splitting can occur.

2 Inserting an oak wedge into the split to try it for size.

3 Pare the ends to fit and apply white glue to the sides before knocking the piece home.

4 and **5** Trim the projections with a small hand saw, which cuts only in straight lines, leaving an uneven edge.

6 Pare the wedge flush with a carving chisel.

7 The finished repair. At this stage of the carving, the repair will serve to show if the wood is still moving as you continue opening up the surface: if the edges hold, the wood has stabilized. For work to be finished naturally – original color, with no staining or polychrome – added wood must be carefully matched in grain direction and color.

Breaks

This is a repair to the crest on a late 17th- or early 18th-century gilded mirror, found in Cairo, but probably French.

1 The clamping points have to be in the same plane, so a little shelf was cut for one end of the clamp. Always dry-assemble before clamping to test that the forces are parallel. This "carvers' clamp" is cut from a sprung steel bedspring and provides very precise positioning.

2 The finished repair from the front. The gilding must now be restored.

Repairing a split in a narrow panel

Here a defect is repaired in a late 17th-century pierced oak pew panel.

1 The carver first opens the split to gauge its size.

2 A piece of oak veneer is cut roughly to size and inserted with white glue.

3 The repair is pared flush with a flat chisel.

4 It is now ready for staining.

Replacement carving

A missing detail – the pendant – is carved and fitted to the mirror (see Breaks).

1 The broken stump is pared with a wide flat chisel to flatten it. The glue to be used is not gap-filling.

2 Testing with a small square.

3 After studying the ornament of the mirror, the carver draws a full-size plan and elevation of the missing pendant.

4 External calipers are used to lay out a small block of basswood, which is then roughly shaped, with the grain running in the same direction as the stump on the frame.

5 The two profiles were drawn on and the piece positioned up before gluing with the aid of the sprung steel clamp; the gluing surface was very slight and would not take much pressure.

6 With the frame in an engineer's vise padded with a cloth, the back of the pendant was carved in until the edges were flush.

7 A block of the right height and curvature was shaped as a cradle to support this now very delicate pendant while the front was carved.

8 The finished replacement is now ready for gesso and gilding (see p. 52).

FINISHING

A completed carving can have a tooled or smoothed finish. Sanding takes away the crispness achieved with sharp tools, but this can sometimes be the effect you want. It is important to remember, however, that if you want to recarve a piece that has been sanded, you must wash it first to remove the fine grit which would otherwise quickly blunt your tools.

Most commercial carvers do not use any form of sanding, because it would be impractical to do so, but an expert restorer working in St. Paul's Cathedral in London has told me that restorers there are convinced that some of the carvings by Grinling Gibbons must have been rubbed with an abrasive – possibly sharkskin, which would not have left any damaging grit.

A carving could simply be left with its tooled or sanded finish, but newly carved wood can soon look grubby if it is not protected from dust and handling. There is a wide range of finishes to choose from, and the demonstrations here show you how to apply some of them. Finishes are also suggested for the different projects in this book, but alternatives may be equally pleasing and valid. A piece of sculpture can look its best just treated with Danish oil and lightly waxed, a bowl could be varnished, a wooden spoon might be left as it is, a relief carving could be painted, and a mirror frame gilded. You could go through the list again and choose an equally good but different finish for most of the items. It can happen that, when you come to the end of a carving, it suggests a different finish from the one you had originally planned. It is worth listening to your carving.

These pictures of the virtually finished woodcarving and the completed project, painted with acrylics and then water-gilded, show how the choice of a finish can transform a piece. The helm was oil-gilded with black gold leaf. (Coat of Arms for Mr. Harris by Antony Denning.)

These two completed versions of Peter Clothier's cat (see p. 160) show the difference between sanding smooth and finishing with gouges.

USING LINSEED OIL

This finish is demonstrated on a Green Man carving, another interpretation of the subject explored in project 12. It had been exhibited in the open air, and the surface had dried out.

1 Raw linseed oil and mineral spirits in a 3:1 ratio were heated in an earthenware pot placed in a saucepan of water. The mineral spirits thin the oil, making it more volatile, and the heat renders it less viscous, aiding its penetration of the wood. Note that the hot oil mixture is highly inflammable and must be handled with care.

2 The mixture was brushed on and left for 10 minutes.

3 Then it was rubbed off hard with a coarse cloth. If simply left on the surface, it would take ages to dry and would readily pick up dirt and fingerprints. The aim is to enhance the wood, which should be smooth and not entirely dry. Repeat the finish as needed. After many applications, the surface will become saturated and extremely durable. It should have a soft glow, not a shine which obscures the forms.

Fuming oak

Fuming ages oak and was the finish chosen for the Green Man mask on p. 166.

1 Clean the surface of pencil marks and grease from your hand, using mineral spirits, denatured alcohol and a gooseneck cabinet scraper.

2 and **3** Remove the mask from the backboard by inserting a wide bevel-edged chisel underneath it and tapping lightly all the way around until the glue and paper seal is broken.

4 Place the mask in a plastic bag ready to be fumed with a 27 percent ammonia solution. You can usually find this at a pharmacy.

5 Pour the ammonia into glazed or enamel containers and quickly insert these around the carving in the bag. This is an unpleasant operation owing to the strength of the fumes; you should wear gloves and a face mask that protects eyes, nose, and

a face mask that protects eyes, nose and mouth. Lift the plastic bag off the surface of the carving with a short stick, because any obstruction of the surface will prevent penetration of the fumes. Seal the bag tightly.

(6) After 3–4 hours retrieve the carving, again wearing your mask. Leave it for half an hour in a well-ventilated space to allow the fumes to disperse. Throw the ammonia down an outside drain followed by a bucket of water.

(7) The fumes react with tannic acid in the oak to produce a weathered grey appearance with an underlying redness, which is revealed by washing the surface with methylated spirits. To create a cooler colour, the wood was stained with dilute Van Dyke crystals (water stain) and sealed, when dry, by brushing with Special Pale Polish. The whole piece was then worked over with grade 1 wire wool to smooth the grain raised by the water stain and lighten the high spots. When the fragments of metal had been brushed out, the surface was waxed again to seal it and render it more visible. Without the polish and wax, the wood would be too absorbent of the subsequent toning.

(8) A dark tone, mixed from lamp black and burnt umber pigment bound in gold size and diluted 3:1 with white spirit, was brushed on and wiped off to create highlights and shadows. When dry, it was again wire-wooled and waxed. As in the carving, this was not a pre-determined idea but adapted to the forms as they emerged.

GILDING

Gilding is an ancient craft requiring patience and practice. It is only possible to outline the process here, so if the finish appeals to you it would be a good idea to get further advice from a class, or an experienced gilder.

You will need specialist equipment and materials: a gilder's tip, cushion and knife, artist's brushes, agate burnisher, pestle and mortar, dibber, fine sieve, double saucepan, bowls or jars, loose gold leaf, whiting, rabbitskin glue, methylated spirit or industrial alcohol, yellow bole, red bole, cotton wool, silk and newspaper.

Rabbitskin glue and parchment size are the traditional sizes for water gilding. Rabbit skin glue is mixed with hot water, so that when cold, it is like firm jelly.

Gesso is a mixture of whiting and rabbitskin glue size. Warm glue and add whiting until the mixture is the consistency of cream. When tested on wood it should give an even cover. Strain through sieve and warm before using.

Bole is a fine clay which comes in various colours. Grind the bole with water and add a little warmed glue size and sieve through a fine mesh. The bole should be opaque but not too thick.

There are basically two methods of gilding: water and oil. Oil is used on textured surfaces and objects exposed to the open air, but it cannot be burnished or distressed. For both oil and water gilding (described here), preparation of the surface is crucial to success.

(1) Apply a thin coat of hot rabbitskin glue and leave overnight to dry.

(2) Apply four to ten layers of blood heat gesso. The hollows will need four coats, the parts to be burnished eight to ten. Before applying a new coat make sure the

gesso is firm but not bone dry. When completed, smooth with a damp soft rag, or finishing paper.

3 Prepare some yellow bole and paint it on warm. Apply several thin coats, allowing it to dry between coats.

4 Paint the parts to be burnished with red bole.

5 Let the bole dry overnight. Brush vigorously with a short-bristled brush. Place a gold leaf on the cushion. Blow gently down to flatten it. Fit your thumb into the loop on the underside of the cushion and hold tip and dibber in the same hand.

6 Cut the gold to convenient size. Brush the tip down the nape of your neck to charge it with static electricity.

7 Place the tip gently but firmly on the gold and lift it up.

8 Hold it in the other hand and wet an area with gilding water (glue, water and alcohol). Lower the tip towards the carving until the leaf is attracted to the wet surface.

9 Press the leaf into position, if necessary, with your dibber. When the water has almost evaporated press the leaf down gently with cotton wool. Overlap leaves by about 3 mm (⅛ in).

10 Allow the piece to dry for between two and six hours. Burnish with a light circular motion over high spots. Increase pressure as shine develops but do not press too hard. When dry remove any loose gold with a sable brush. The finished gilding can be left as it is, or, some areas can be toned down with a little thin colour, rabbitskin glue or artists' matt varnish, or the piece can be distressed to make the gold look old and worn.

GALLERY

BOXES

SPOONS

BOWLS

RELIEF

MASKS

LETTERS

CHIP CARVING

CARVING IN THREE
DIMENSIONS

FRAMES

Boxes

Wooden boxes are useful objects and can take almost any form. They can be simple and unadorned, deriving their effect from the beauty of the wood and the maker's skills, or they can be decorated in a multitude of ways, from lacquering to painted patterns and pictures, from inlaying and marquetry to carved ornament. The carved decoration is as varied as its designers and can range from chip carved patterns through low relief to quite complex pictorial work. Carved as gifts or for sale, conceived as sculptures or containers, many boxes are so attractive that they become collectable items in their own right. The illustrations on these pages show some successful and widely differing approaches to these endlessly appealing objects.

Monkey box
Phil Poole

A glass pane has been set behind the fretted design on the top of this mahogany box. The relief carving has been kept very low and simple, but a great deal of information is subtly and convincingly conveyed.

13½ × 10 × 3½ inches

Trinket box
Charles MacEachern

In contrast to the Monkey box, the relief carving on this example in teak comes well above the surface of the lid, as though the prehistoric sea creatures are lying on it. It would be possible to use a router to hollow out the inside shape, but here a hole was cut right through and a base was set in.

2 × 6¾ × 7½ inches

Carved wooden boxes
Jonathan Mushlin

These fascinating little boxes demonstrate a very individual sculptural approach. When closed, they could easily be mistaken for small abstract sculptures.

Approx. 3 inches long

Spoons

Wooden spoons are normally thought of as utilitarian items which should be plain in shape and easy to clean. Some patterns may be carved on a handle, but they are generally considered impractical. Salad utensils are more likely to be decorated because they are intended to grace the dining table, and their function is less demanding.

Otherwise, spoons that are embellished with carving are those designed as decorative or symbolic objects rather than for culinary purposes, and their origins often reach back into the mists of time. One of the best known of these is the Welsh love spoon. Once carved with whittling knives by lonely shepherds during the long winter evenings, many are now churned out for the tourist trade, but the best are made by carvers for whom the motifs have retained their symbolic importance. A few examples of those beautifully carved spoons are shown here.

Love spoon
Norman Vessey

_____

This decorative triple spoon was carved from a single piece of pine and then stained. It incorporates traditional motifs, following one of several typical Welsh love spoon patterns. Virtually any wood is suitable for those purely ornamental spoons – elm, sycamore, and yew have all been used.

7 × 9 inches

Love spoon
Wendy Rees

_____

The theme of this spoon is "love – rare and beautiful," illustrated by the kingfisher, an uncommon and exquisite bird, which bears a rosebud as a gift of love. The spoon is finely carved in yew and finished with wax. Notice the punch marks used to give texture to the background.

11 × 4½ inches

Love spoon
Wendy Rees

_____

This delicate spoon carved in yew symbolizes the fragility of love and the mutual guiding of two people in love. The ring in the shepherd's crook was carved from the same solid piece of wood as the rest of the spoon. The finished piece was waxed.

12 × 2 inches

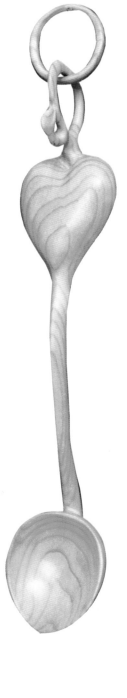

Bowls

Wooden bowls, like boxes and spoons, are first and foremost functional objects. But provided they fit their purpose, they can take on a great variety of size and shape, from almost flat to very deep and from circular through ovals of differing proportions to almost rectangular — not to mention asymmetrical forms. The surface treatment can be equally varied, although patterns are more commonly carved than pictorial subjects. Many bowls are left plain, relying on their shapes, the grain of the wood, and their tactile qualities to please the senses; others are richly painted with floral or other motifs. Those illustrated here show just a few of the countless possible approaches.

Two bowls
Paul Caton

Carved in "green" cherry – freshly cut, unseasoned wood – these two bowls have a beautiful tactile quality. They rely entirely on their shapes and the patterns in the grain of the wood for their beauty.

18-inch diameter × 8 inches high

Four-cornered bowl
Dick Onians

This lovely large bowl was carved from the wood of an apple tree brought down in a devastating storm that hit southern Britain in October 1987. The bowl is a beautiful abstract form as well as a functional object, and it is no surprise to learn that the carver is primarily a sculptor.

12 × 20 × 17 inches

Holly leaf bowl
*Helen Cumberlidge and
Roderick Jenkinson*

———

*This wonderfully carved bowl
captures the qualities of a holly
leaf with strikingly true-to-life
effect.*

13½ × 8½ inches

Beech leaves in hornbeam
*Helen Cumberlidge
and
Roderick Jenkinson*

———

*The inspiration for
this carving came
from plant fossils
exposed in rock. The
shape was first
turned on a lathe,
and then the beech
leaves were carved
into part of the
surface, as though
revealed by the
peeling away of a
thin layer of the
hornbeam.*

*Approx. 15-inch diameter ×
approx. 3½ inches deep*

Bowl with handles
Paul Caton

———

*There is usually very little
grain pattern in basswood,
so this bowl must rely on its
pleasing proportions.
Gouge marks have been
allowed to remain on the
inside, giving a contrast of
texture made apparent by
light and touch.*

16-inch diameter × 7 inches high

Relief

Carving in relief can be used to create works of art in their own right, or to embellish other objects. In the preceding pages, we have seen it employed on boxes, spoons, and bowls. It can also be used effectively for the decoration of frames and other furniture, and even for buildings. A relief carving may be hardly more than a drawing and exploit the same devices to convey an impression of depth, or it can be so deeply carved as to appear fully three-dimensional. The carving can be pierced to create a screen or the illusion of a free-standing object, or it can be carved against a background, which may be plain or form an integral part of the design. In a pictorial subject, the whole range of depths frequently occurs in the same work. These pages illustrate some of the myriad forms that relief carving can take.

Egyptian candlestick
Charles MacEachern

The intriguing relief on this beautifully carved candlestick gives it a three-dimensional quality – you want to turn it around to see what happens on the hidden parts. The carving, in teak, is glued to a separate base.

3¾ × 8 inches

Coat of arms of the Duke of Norfolk
John Roberts

Carved in basswood for the Fishmongers' Company in London, this is a high-quality coat of arms. Though all the heraldic elements have to be correct, there is still freedom in the design, which is what makes coats of arms interesting to carve. In the past, the painting, gilding, and lettering were done by others, but now the carver often does all these tasks, as here.

Approx. 32 × 26 inches

"Give Us This Day"
Bon Rasmussen

A marvelous cornucopia, spilling out fruit and vegetables. The design, made to fit into a long, narrow shape, has been cleverly worked out and is enhanced by the bold color.

10 × 42 inches

Feasting in a pear tree
Bon Rasmussen

Inspired by watching all the creatures he has depicted feeding in the old pear tree outside his studio, the carver has fashioned this screen from a single piece of walnut, finished with raw linseed oil. The simple carving style combined with piercing makes a very effective piece.

30 × 1 × 60 inches

Vouivre Parisienne
Antony Denning

This little French wyvern, or fabulous serpent, is an example of a relief carving which appears to be three-dimensional, but is designed to rest against a wall, so that the back is not carved. Because it is made of basswood, the surface textures do not have to compete with an obvious grain pattern. The inspiration for the piece was an illustration by Joyce Hargreaves from Hargreaves' New Illustrated Bestiary.

7½ inches high

Stiff leaf carving
Michael Lewis

————

This piece follows closely a stone-carved design on the 13th-century west front of Wells Cathedral in south-western England. The leaves and stems, carved in the style known as "stiff leaf," have been formed into a symmetrical design which fills the pointed arch to perfection. Subtle undercutting adds to the three-dimensional quality.

17½ × 18½ inches

Fly Fishing
Rodney Smith

————

This carving of a scene in the Cairngorms Mountains of northeastern Scotland shows a high degree of technical accomplishment.

21 × 15 × 5 inches

Masks

Most people have seen examples of the strange and often powerful masks used in the performance of ritual dances and ceremonies, processions and carnivals. Whether they are simple or grotesque, their purpose is to alter the appearance and even the character of the wearer. But not all masks are intended to be worn. From early times, masks have been used on furniture and buildings, carved as part of a decorative scheme, or hung singly on a wall. Unlike masks for wear, these need not be hollowed out and can be as small as you choose. Both kinds of mask are frequently derived from the human face, like those shown here, but animals, including birds and fish, are also popular subjects.

Mask
Letizia MacRae Brown

A superbly carved and simply treated plain mask in basswood. It has a classical stillness and a definite presence. It demonstrates that a subject need not be complicated to be effective.

10 × 6 inches

Mask for an ochlocrat
Antony Denning

Carved in elm, then stained and waxed, this mask, which combines profile and front views, owes an obvious debt to African masks and to Picasso, but is an imitation of neither.

Approx. 15 inches high

Green man
John Roberts

Fitted into an almost square diamond, this walnut mask is carved in an English Gothic style, but is a strongly individual piece, showing how traditional elements can be distilled into a carver's own style.

16 inches diagonally

Letters

Most people can learn to cut letters with chisels and gouges, but creating the subtly shaped letters and sensitive spacing that make a well-designed inscription requires more skills. Many letter cutters become totally dedicated to the refinement of their craft, and the results can be immensely satisfying. The inscriptions here give some idea of what the most skillful can achieve, but it is a good idea to study as many lettering examples as you can. By observing and comparing inscriptions, you can begin to pick out the features that distinguish the gifted from the mundane, and so develop an eye for good lettering just as you might improve your ear by listening to many interpretations of the same music.

"Raise the Stone"
Martin Wenham

Like the raised alphabet, this is sculpture. The informal slender capital letters are incised in beech and finished with wax.

Letters 2½ inches high

Alphabet in relief
Michael Harvey

This bold raised-letter alphabet in Parana pine is a piece of sculpture. A bandsaw was used to cut the outline shape and a router to make the deeply carved internal shapes designed to cast strong shadows. The shapes were finished with chisels and gouges, and the wood and Welsh slate base were treated with beeswax.

14 × 5¼ × 1¼ inches

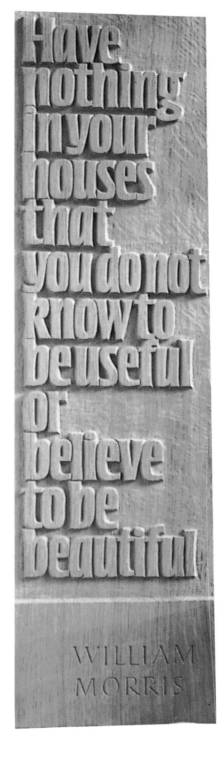

Quotation from William Morris (1834–96)
Michael Harvey

This quotation was carved in English oak for an exhibition held at the University of Texas to commemorate the 150th anniversary of poet and master-craftsman William Morris's birth. The letters were carved with chisels and gouges after removal of the waste with a router. The background was finished with a flattish gouge, and the surface of the letters was finely sanded. The whole piece was then waxed.

18 × 5 inches

An alphabet for a child with initials L.M.
Michael Harvey

These letters were incised with gouges and chisels in Parana pine, then painted and varnished. Although finely drawn and cut, they were designed to withstand the rough and tumble of play. It was just a happy chance that the child's initials followed each other in the alphabet.

14½ inches high × 5⁵⁄₁₆ × 1½ inches

Bread platter
Martin Wenham

Designing an inscription to follow the perimeter of a circle poses a tricky problem because the letters have less space at their bases. It is worth studying this piece to see how admirably it has been resolved. The design was incised in cherry wood and finished with olive oil.

Letters 1⅛ inch high

Chip carving

Like whittling, chip carving probably began as a pleasant way of passing the time while also decorating everyday furniture and utensils. Many of the apparently complex patterns which evolved were based upon relatively simple geometrical constructions. Once those were mastered, the more adventurous carvers could invent their own designs, which sometimes became quite pictorial, showing stylized birds, flowers, animals, and occasionally even people. Lettering often occurs as well, and it is not unknown for contemporary professional letter cutters to favor the use of chip carving knives. The technique can be adapted to modern subjects, but over-realistic pictorial designs tend to be unsuccessful. Though usually carved with knives, some of the cuts on 18th- and 19th-century examples must have been made with gouges. Nowadays, chisels and gouges are often used, and cutting the patterns provides excellent practice in the control of tools.

Bread board
Dick Onians

This effective rosette pattern is based upon quite simple geometrical constructions. The wood is carved with chisels and gouges rather than the traditional chip carving knives. The carver uses this sort of design to show students the shapes which can be made by individual gouges.

8 × 10 inches

Platter
Peter Clothier

An excellent example of the contemporary use of a traditional chip carving pattern, skillfully executed in basswood.

6 × 6 inches

Carving in three dimensions

Carving in three dimensions poses particular problems for the artist carver or sculptor because the piece has to be a satisfactory composition from all viewing angles. Although there are artists who deliberately design around a favored viewing angle, and a piece will invariably work better from some angles than from others, it should still normally have a quality which will stimulate the spectator to move around it and experience it as a complete object. With small carvings these considerations become less significant because it is possible to take in the whole object very quickly. In a strictly representational carving, such as that of a bird, for instance, it will matter less still, because the viewer will be concentrating on the accuracy of detail with which the creature's likeness has been carved and painted. Where the piece is a work of imagination, the form itself will provide the interest and will be correspondingly more important. The illustrations here cover an interesting variety of approaches.

Cormorant box
Nicola Henshaw

This carver spends a great deal of her time observing and sketching animals and birds. The wings of this lovely cormorant are a hinged lid which opens to reveal a crop full of wooden fish.
15¾ × 9⅞ × 19¾ inches

Apples
Peter Clothier

Fruit are challenging objects to carve, and here the carver has managed to convey the qualities of apples and wood.
4 inches

Diana and Actaeon
John Roberts

This beautiful carving in oak has to be walked around to be fully appreciated.
30 inches high

Figurehead HMS Gannet
Paul Stevens

Carved in Russian
pine and decorated
with yacht paints,
this is a magnificent
continuation of the
great figurehead
tradition.

*Overall length approx.
60 inches*

Female eider
Philip Nelson

A fine waterfowl
sculpture carved in
basswood, textured
with a pyrograph (a
wood-burning tool),
and painted with
acrylics.

Approx. 12¾ inches long

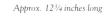

Family group
Ferelyth Wills

This small group,
carved in cherry
wood, is designed to
be constantly
rearranged, ensuring
that its tactile
qualities will be
appreciated.

*Five pieces. Heights approx.
3 inches, 3 inches, 4 inches,
5 inches, and 8 inches*

Girl with plaits
Ferelyth Wills

A stylized and satisfying small mahogany sculpture based upon a girl reading, but transformed into an almost abstract form.

Approx. 20 inches high

Masquerading figure
Ross Fuller

This striking sculpture carved in basswood, gessoed and painted with egg tempera and oil glazes, expresses the duality of the sheep and the wolf in human nature.

15 × 5 × 9 inches

"Discontinuity"
Dick Onians

This intriguing sculpture, carved in poplar, was inspired by the concept of carving a dotted line.

19 × 2¾ × 2¾ inches

Frames

Impressive paintings and mirrors are often surrounded by beautifully carved and gilded frames. But the frame for a painting should not be so elaborate that it claims more attention than the picture. It must enhance the painting without being obtrusive. Mirror frames are different because their images are fleeting and could be said to complement them. Like a stage they only fulfill their function when the actors appear. A mirror frame can, therefore, assert itself and offers the carver greater freedom of expression. The illustrations here can act as starters to set your imagination to work.

The Attic Window
Antony Denning

When this enlarged detail from a painting needed framing, the frame was designed to take the place of the rest of the picture. A Dutch gable was adapted to create the shape, and a window inserted. The pigeon was cut out with a jig saw, then carved and painted. The ready-made balls were gessoed and water gilded. The rest of the frame was stained and thinly coated with flat varnish.

30 inches high

Oak leaves mirror frame
Lynn Hodgson

Leaves and acorns have been wrought into a stylized design which fits the simple rectangular frame to make a satisfying piece. It was carved in burl oak and finished with Danish oil.

12 × 18 inches

The man in the moon mirror frame
Peter Clothier

This witty frame looks deceptively simple. You need very sharp tools to carve as cleanly as this in pine.
12 inches

Walnut frame
Ross Fuller

This frame is based upon an original from about 1740 in the Victoria & Albert Museum in London. The carver spent a lot of time taking measurements, making drawings, and taking photographs from which to work. It is a very complex three-dimensional piece, but the final result is brilliant because it has so much life and energy. A danger with copies is that they will be accurate but lifeless.
23 × 16 × 7 inches

PRACTICAL WOODCARVING

· **OBJECTIVE** · · · · · · · · · · · · · · · · · · ·

To gain more experience in using carving tools by making a woodcut that will produce an attractive print.

PICTORIAL WOODCUT

The most enjoyable way to practice new skills is by making something worthwhile. A woodcut enables you to extend your control of your tools by carving into a flat surface as you did with the blanks (see p. 42) while creating a block that you can use to print multiple patterns or a single subject on paper or fabric.

The Chinese were making woodcuts as long ago as the 7th century A.D., and there are occasional European examples dating from the 12th century, but it was only after the development of printing in the 15th century that they were used extensively in the West. The great German painter and engraver Albrecht Dürer (1471-1528) was the first artist to make the blocks, print and publish his own books, (e.g. *Apocalypse*, 1498). In the early days of printing, letters were carved, so it was logical to create the illustrations in the same way. All the wood-blocks were made to a standard thickness, "type high." The block was usually a piece of softwood cut plankwise with the grain running parallel with the longer edge (you can often see traces of the grain in the print). Woodcuts were largely superseded by copper engravings until the fine natural history illustrations of the English artist Thomas Bewick (1753–1828), who had begun his career as a metal engraver, turned wood engraving into an art form and renewed interest in wood as a material from which to print.

A wood engraving differs from a woodcut in that the block is cut from boxwood across the grain, and lines are engraved in the end grain using gravers or burins normally associated with copper engraving. Both woodcuts and wood engravings make relief prints, so the parts you cut away are white and the parts you leave uncarved print black. If you want a black line, you have to carve away the wood on each side of it. On copper engravings, the engraved line retains the ink and prints black; the pressure needed for this intaglio process would soon destroy a wood block.

Although it is thought that woodcuts were originally made with

TOOLS AND MATERIALS

For carving:
- Specialized woodcut tools: No. 9 Gouge; No. 11 Veiner; No. 39 V tool
OR
Chisels, gouges, and V tools (straight or bent) from basic toolkit
- Bench hook
- Any softwood or basswood
For printing:
- Plastic board (or glass sheet)
- One or two rubber rollers 4–6 in
- Palette knife (or old table knife)
- Old spoon (optional)
- Paper for printing
- Newspaper
- Printing ink
- Cleaning solvent

knives, like chip carving (see p. 88), they are now usually produced with small gouges which nestle in the hand and are comfortable to push. Apart from their size, these tools are the same as carving gouges, which can easily be used instead.

DESIGN CONSIDERATIONS

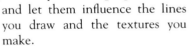

Designing a woodcut is much the same as composing any black and white drawing. Your aim is to make your picture or pattern a balance of black and white, which does not imply the same quantity of each. Large areas of black or white, thin black lines, fine white lines, and all sorts of textures can be experimented with. The tools used lend a distinctive character to a woodcut, so keep the shapes of the gouges in mind and let them influence the lines you draw and the textures you make.

Remember that the design you cut in the wood will print the opposite way around. Look at its reflection in a mirror to see how it will come out. If it is important for the print to be the same way around as the original drawing (where there are letters or numbers, for example), you must reverse the drawing when transferring it to the block. An easy way to do this is to place a piece of carbon paper, black side up, under your sheet while you are drawing.

PLAN

Make a tracing from your actual size drawing. Turn it over and go over the lines with a very soft pencil.

WOODCUTTING TOOLS

Woodcutting tools are usually under 3 inches long, and tend to have comfortable mushroom-shaped handles with one side flattened to stop them from rolling off the table, and so that you can cut at a low angle.

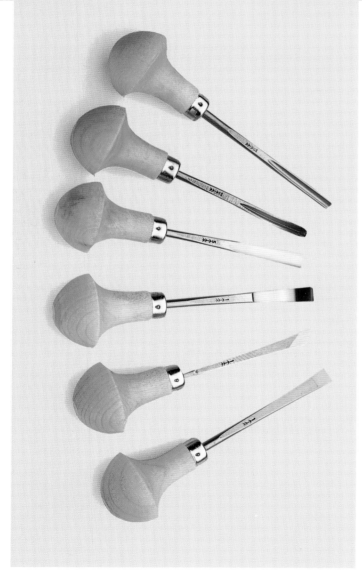

METHOD

Any wood can be used, but softwoods and basswood are the most common choices. Hardwoods other than basswood can be difficult and tiring for this purpose. Some artists use plywood and chipboard, but these are very hard on the edges of the tools. Linoleum is a popular alternative, because it is eventextured and easy to cut, especially if warmed, but you cannot take as many prints from a linoleum block as from a woodblock. Plane the wood smooth, but do not sand it, because grit from sandpaper will remain in the wood and quickly blunt your tools. Whether you are using specific woodcutting tools or those from your toolkit, you will probably find the V, the U, and the semicircular shapes the most useful.

For printing, you will need a flat surface on which to roll out the ink. This could be a sheet of glass, a marble slab, or some plastic-coated chipboard. Rubber rollers are the easiest means of spreading the ink and taking the print, but you can use an old spoon for the printing instead. Newsprint is good for trials, but make your final print on a quality paper that is not too heavily sized and is less likely to yellow with age. There is a variety of papers and inks specially made for printmaking, so see what is available locally and experiment. Oilbased inks make better prints than water-based, but create more mess. Spread newspaper around generously, and clean the tools and block after printing, using a solvent such as mineral spirits for oil-based inks.

Stage one

1 Some artists like to draw their design directly on the wood, often using a brush and ink to give bold areas of black and white and exclude any fiddly elements. Another method is to transfer your original drawing with carbon paper or by tracing, as here. Trace the drawing, turn the tracing over, and go over the lines with a very soft pencil.

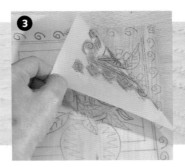

2 Turn the tracing the right way up again, attach it firmly to your block of wood with masking tape, and scribble over the lines.

3 Keeping the rest of the paper in position, peel back a corner to check if the imprint is clear. If it is not, you will either have to go over the line on the back again or substitute some carbon paper and draw on the line with a hard pencil. If all is well, continue transferring the remainder of the drawing. When the process is complete, remove the tracing paper and strengthen any faint lines. You have now reached the point illustrated left.

Stage two

4 You can shade the parts that are to print black, or paint them with brush and ink, because it is surprisingly easy to cut across an area if you have only a line and your memory to guide you.

5 When you are ready to start carving, put your wood-block on a bench hook. You must be able to move the block so that you are always cutting away from yourself. Your spare hand can be used to steady the wood while the bench hook takes the pressure of the tools. Select an appropriate tool, such as the gouge for this area of white. Begin with the larger areas and proceed to the detail.

6 It is possible to carve very thin lines with a chisel, but they tend to fill with ink and need cleaning out after a few prints.

First stage
The drawing has been transferred to the wood.

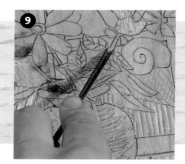

7, **8**, and **9** Choose the gouges that will cut the required width of line or produce a texture like that behind the vase. The illustrations below show stages in cutting the block.

Stage three
When you think the block is finished, do a test print. If you are happy with it, make as many prints as you wish. If not, clean the block, carve your alterations, and print again.

10 and **11** When printing, place newspaper over a much larger area than you think you will need. Put your inking slab on the newspaper and squeeze some printing ink onto the surface. Spread the ink with an old table knife or palette knife.

12 Work the rubber roller in different directions to create a thin, even layer that is tacky, but not too sticky.

Second stage
Woodcut in different stages of development.

13 Place the wood-block close to the slab and roll a film of ink all over it. Make sure of complete coverage by rolling in every direction, picking up more ink from the slab if necessary, but be careful not to apply the ink too thickly. Your block is now ready to print.

Third stage

The carving is complete. The block has been inked and then cleaned.

Stage four

14 If you have plenty of space, move the block to a clean area of newspaper. (If not, make sure the newspaper around the block is clean.) Carefully place a sheet of printing paper over it and gently press it onto the inked block.

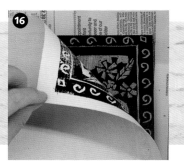

15 The paper must not move once it is in position, so hold it and the block steady with one hand while you pass a clean roller all over the back of the sheet, moving your hand to a new spot when necessary.

16 Carefully pull back a corner to see how the block is printing. If you think it needs more rolling, it is easy to let the corner return and to continue. If the print looks all right, peel off the entire sheet and set it aside to dry on some clean newspaper. The first few prints are sometimes a bit patchy due to uneven absorption of the ink, but after that they are usually good and black.

17 Instead of using a roller for printing, you can rub the back of the paper with a metal spoon. Either the handle or the bowl could be suitable, depending on the shape of the spoon. This is usually slower than working with a roller, but can give high-quality prints.

18 When printing is finished, clean the block with water or the appropriate solvent. Your block will now appear as shown on p. 79, ready for re-use whenever required. If you enjoy making woodcuts, you might like to experiment with multiple patterns or making color prints with more than one block. A specialized book on printmaking, such as Running Press's *Encyclopedia of Printmaking Techniques*, will describe the techniques you need for lining up paper and block so that the print registers in the same place each time.

Fourth stage
You may need to apply more ink in order to achieve even printing. Clean the block carefully when finished.

Vase of flowers
Lucinda Denning

The design is simple, but effective, with strong black and white contrasts.

PROJECT

2

To carve an opener with a subtle but effective pattern in low relief on the handle and a simply shaped blade.

LETTER OPENER

odern packaging often seems designed to defeat ordinary attempts to breach its defenses, and letters too can benefit from an implement sharp enough to secure an entry without damaging the contents. A wooden letter opener is the perfect tool for the task.

DESIGN CONSIDERATIONS

There is no necessity in this design for the carving to exceed ¹⁄₁₆ inch in depth. Of course, it will not matter if you cut more deeply, but aim for ¹⁄₁₆ inch. Technically, because it is carved on both sides and the design does follow around from one side to the other, it is a three-dimensional object, but from the carver's point of view, it is a very low relief carving which has to be done twice.

The handle of this letter opener was copied from an antique ivory knife (right) which was probably used for the uncut pages of books and for broadsheets. The strap and buckle made a satisfying design immanently suitable for the purpose. I altered the shape of the blade to give it the finer point necessary for opening envelopes. The blade should have a fairly thin edge and a pointed tip. Comfort is less important than in some other knives, because the letter opener is unlikely to be used continuously over long periods, nor with a lot of pressure, but the handle should be pleasant to hold as well as attractive.

Existing designs are helpful in getting you thinking about blends of shape and pattern. When trying out this design, I initially left out the thin line which runs around the strap parallel with the edge, but including this decorative feature helped to carry the eye around the end of the handle, and made the strap far more convincing.

The only drawing you will need is a plan. It is worth making a template of the overall shape, especially if you are carving more than one opener; cut out a thin point to indicate the position of the spike on the tongue of the buckle. It is certainly useful to have a template showing the shape of the strap and the inside rim of the

TOOLS AND MATERIALS

- Basic toolkit
- Try square
- Small straight chisel maximum 3 mm (⅛ in) wide
- Gouge No. 9 or 10 straight 2 mm (¹⁄₁₆ in)
- Spokeshave (optional)
- Cabinet scraper
- Beech, yew, boxwood, or other hardwood

buckle (see right), because you may want to check or re-draw after you have started carving. Make a template by putting carbon paper under your drawing and duplicating it directly onto thin poster board, or transfer it with the aid of tracing paper. If you can get ahold of some of the transparent plastic used by stonemasons for their templates, you can trace straight onto that.

The design has been adapted from this old ivory letter opener. The handle is essentially the same, but the blade has been modified.

PLANS

Divide some paper or poster board into squares and enlarge the drawings below to make templates (see pp. 19–20).

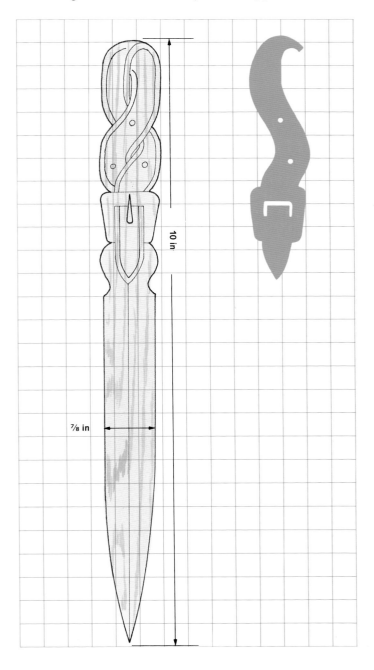

10 in

⁷/₈ in

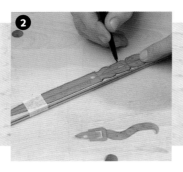

METHOD

Though you can use any wood, it is best to choose one that is likely to form a lasting edge. This letter opener is made from a scrap of beech, which is quite close-grained and hard, but boxwood would be excellent, and any hardwood would be worth trying. Of the softwoods, yew would be a good choice. The piece for the knife measured approximately $10 \times \frac{7}{8} \times \frac{1}{4}$ inch after being planed.

You will not need all the basic tools, but it is easier to have the kit available, taking out each tool as you require it and keeping it out until the work is finished. Remember to note carefully how the tools are held in the photographs.

Stage one

1. Draw the center line along one side of the wood, down each end and along the other side. Then draw the center line along each edge and across the ends.

2. If you are using a template for the complete opener, align it on one side of the wood, and tape it into position with masking tape. Draw around the template and mark the position of the spike. A black pen has been used for clarity, but normally this would be done with a soft pencil. Remove the template and use a try square to draw lines across at the following points: where the strap crosses; at the top and bottom of the buckle; and across the top of the blade. Carry these lines down the edges and across the other side.

3. The handle template has to be used one way up to draw the strap crossing and the other way up to draw the quick turn at the top of the handle. It can be used either way up to draw the inner sides of the buckle and the end of the strap. The lines will have to be joined and adjusted by eye because the template is only a guide. Now draw the opener in the same way on the other side of the wood. You have now reached the stage illustrated below.

Stage two

4. Secure the piece with a padded clamp (p. 39) and, with a chisel, carefully cut vertically down across the edges to set in the profile of the strap and buckle. Some woods have a tendency to split as you near the bottom of the cut, so you may have to cut halfway, turn the opener over, and carve down from the other side. If you have a spare piece, it is a good idea to do a test cut. An alternative is to hold the wood on edge in a vise and cut with the grain from each side of each indent toward its deepest part.

First stage
The design is being drawn on both sides of the wood.

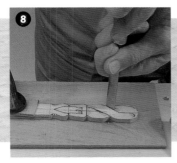

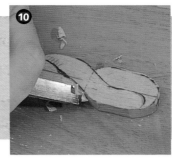

5 When you come to the concave curve at the top of the blade, use a gouge of the equivalent shape. If you have no straight or fishtail gouge of the right sweep, you can improvise with a bent or salmon bent gouge, even if this is not ideal.

6 Move the clamp and set in the shape of the blade in the same way. A carpenter's chisel is being used here, but a carver's chisel would be equally good, or, as in step 4, the opener can be held on edge in a vise and the shape shaved away with a chisel or spokeshave. You have now reached the point illustrated below.

Stage three

7 As you will have carved away much of the center line around the edge, you should re-draw

it. Keeping one finger against the wood as a guide you can quickly run a line around connecting any bits of the original marking which remain.

8 Set in the lines of the strap and buckle by pushing vertically downward. The carving needs only to be about $1/16$ inch deep, though it will not matter if you go a little deeper in places. Then, to start shaping the strap, hold the chisel or gouge at a low angle and push into the wood toward the vertical cuts you have just made, thus removing a thin wedge.

9 On the quick turn at the end of the handle, slice around the curve while pushing forward.

10 Carve away thin wedge shapes from the areas where one part of the strap appears to weave under another, and gradually add a slight curve to the top surface of the strap. Keep the depth of cut constant along the line at the top of the buckle, but where the strap crosses over itself, the outer edges should be slightly deeper than the inside, and the quick curve at the top should be marginally deeper on the inside than on the outside. The small chisel will be needed to shape the strap and inside of the buckle on each side of the

spike. The buckle itself slopes gently toward the blade, to give a little depth for the spike and a bit more for the strap. The curved part between blade and buckle also turns down to meet the buckle. The rounding of the corners and edges of the buckle, and the slight curve on the outside edges of the strap make the handle comfortable to hold, and can be achieved with any chisels or gouges which suit.

Second stage
The basic form of the opener has been established.

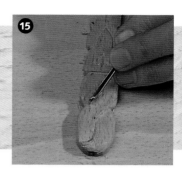

11 The hole in the strap through which the spike of the buckle appears is made by pushing in a very small, No. 9 or 10 gouge at a steep angle. With the same tool used almost flat, shave a little off the top of the spike to meet the cut you have just made, thus shaping the top of the spike at the same time.

12 Prepare to shape the blade by placing a length of wood under the opener before clamping the handle. This will support the blade and give you room to maneuver a chisel or spokeshave. Remove quite a thin shaving with each stroke. Your aim is to make slight curves on the "flat" side of the blade, both from side to side and down toward the tip. These curves should form a continuous shape which ends a fraction above the center line.

13 Leave the opener on its support or take it down to bench level again to finish the blade with a cabinet scraper.

14 The final touches to the handle are to tidy up the edges of the strap, draw the fine line inside the strap edge, make the tightening holes, and carve a shallow concave scoop between the pointed end of the strap and the buckle. Begin with the scoop, working inward from each side, across the grain, with a very slightly curved gouge, which gives a little movement to the end of the strap. Then, using your V tool and pressing lightly, follow the lines of the strap edges, shaving them slightly and making a faint indent where the strap crosses. This will finish the edges and crossing points and help make the strap look continuous. Make sure that you are not cutting against the grain. On the strap above the buckle, work in from the outside to the center. On the quick curve at the top, work away from the center of the curve in each direction. Work toward the point of the strap from the thick end of the spike and toward the top of the buckle from there up. If there is a slight V groove in places where it is unwanted, it is not too difficult to shave it away.

15 Draw a guideline with a soft pencil just inside the edges of the strap and then use your V tool to cut the thinnest line you can. The little holes for tightening the strap were drilled right through the original ivory; you can do the same, or drill or carve a hole part of the way. The illustration below left shows the carving at this stage, virtually finished on one side. When you have carved both sides, check the opener from all angles and make any adjustments to the shapes which you consider necessary before finishing.

Third stage
One side of the opener is virtually finished. You will now need to carve the other side.

Finishing

The completed handle was rubbed with very fine sandpaper to make it reasonably comfortable to hold. The dust was then washed off with some mineral spirits and the opener was given a coat of light oak stain. This is not essential, but it adds contrast and helps the carving to show up better. By the time the stain has faded, the opener will have acquired some patina. It needs to be protected from dirt and handling with an oil, such as Danish oil, or a varnish. Flat polyurethane varnish was chosen here so that the letter opener would not look too shiny.

Letter opener
Antony Denning

The finished opener is both functional and attractive.

. . . . **OBJECTIVE** . . . .

To become familiar with a different carving technique for which the traditional tools are knives, but which can equally well be done with chisels.

CHIP CARVING

Chip carving is an ancient craft used for the embellishment of everyday articles from butter molds and bread boards to furniture and even parts of buildings. Museums often display chests, cradles, and other objects decorated in this way. Chip carving is a straightforward, relatively shallow-cut technique, using few tools. Many of the patterns are based on simple geometry, but are very effective.

Chip carving consists of a series of two or three linked, angled cuts, usually made with the tip of a knife, which release a clean chip of wood and reveal a V-bottomed groove or a trifaceted hole.

Two knives only are needed: a chip knife and a stab knife. You can choose these from among the knives you have available, depending on your individual taste and hand size. In the past when sailors and shepherds decorated objects like Welsh lovespoons to while away the hours, pen- or clasp knives were commonly used.

DESIGN CONSIDERATIONS

It is probably a good idea to start with geometric designs, but you certainly need not be limited to them. Many of the examples in museums have stylized but quite freely drawn plants and animals as well as abstract patterns. My own feeling is that attempts to be naturalistic are not very successful, but you can study traditional motifs based upon natural forms and adopt the principles of stylization to make your own designs. In this way, it is possible to use any subject – even cars, airplanes, and buildings – as the basis of new designs. In this project the carver has taken a design from a 16th-century box and has modified it only slightly. It is useful to make a careful drawing with ruler and compasses on paper before transferring it to the wood.

TOOLS AND MATERIALS
- Chip knife
- Stab knife
- Draftsman's pencil
- Ruler
- Compasses (screw adjustment)
- Dividers (curved surfaces)
- Try-squares (right angles)
- Pencil eraser (optional)
- Fine sandpaper
- Any easily carved wood (not pine)

PLAN

Enlarge this pattern onto paper first. Draw the concentric circles. Keep the radius of the innermost circle to construct the design within. To find the six points walk the compasses or dividers round the circle. Use these points as centers for drawing the arcs which make the petals. By continuing the arcs outside the circle you can find the centers for the inward curves in the bases of the triangles.

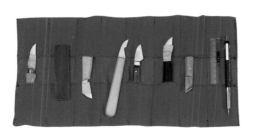

A homemade tool roll containing a selection of knives, a fine sharpening stone, ruler, and draftsman's mechanical pencil. The carver's favorite chip knife is on the left.

SAMPLERS

These basswood samplers show the versatility of patterns you can try for chip carving.
1 Simple stab and chip patterns.
2 Some slightly more complicated patterns, but still using the basic techniques described in the project.
3 A design composed of triangular chips. Notice damage due to vulnerable "short" grain.
4 An attractive pattern derived from circles and a simple V cut grid.
5 Edge detail suggesting how chip carving might enhance an otherwise plain household item.
6 A selection of patterns on which to practice your techniques.

1

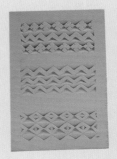

2

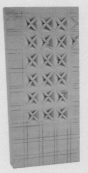

3

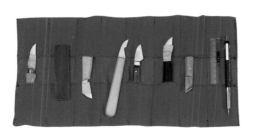

4

5

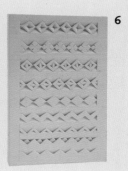

6

HOLDING

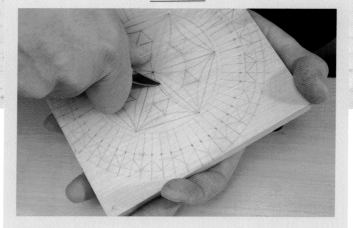

The wood is traditionally held in the carver's free hand and rotated after each cut, presenting the next line to be carved. In this way, the knife hand is always working in the same direction and the grip need not be altered. Hold the chip knife as though you were about to spread butter – edge toward the thumb and first finger wrapped around the handle.

METHOD

A chip knife does not need a large blade, since only the point is used, but small blades tend to be thin and liable to bend. A blade measuring 1–1½ inches, taped with masking tape to leave ⅜ inch of the tip showing should work well. Flat-sided wooden handles give the best control – a round handle can twist in your grip.

The stab knife, which makes graduating perpendicular cuts, is similar to a skew chisel and should have a straight blade 1 inch long and ½ inch wide, with the cutting edge sloping back at about 45° from the tip. Sharpen the chip knife to give a 10° bevel and the stab knife to a 30° bevel. You will find details of how to sharpen your knives on p. 37.

The old lovespoons were often carved from fruit wood, such as pear, probably when the wood was slightly green and much easier to cut – an essential quality for chip carving. Basswood, with its even grain, is an excellent choice, and birch is good, though not always available. Jelutong works well, but has a tendency to flake on "short" grain, and pine can be difficult due to hard and soft grain layers – not good for beginners. The best advice is to try sample cuts on any available wood.

Cutting techniques

During cutting, your thumb is always in contact with the wood and the knuckle of the first finger also rubs on the surface, aiding control of the knife in the depth and angle of cutting. Draw the tip of the knife through the surface by pressing the outside edge of your thumb, by the nail, onto the wood and then "closing" your hand toward the thumb, taking the knife along the cutting line ¼ inch at a time. Move the thumb forward another ¼ inch, close the hand again, and so on. Cuts usually start shallow, deepen to the middle and become shallow again toward the end. The tip of the knife must be able to move easily through the wood: if it cuts too deeply or if the blade is dull, it is likely to jump or jam and may cause injury. The gap between the masked blade and your thumb should never exceed ¼ inch to limit the danger if the knife does jump forward and cut you.

The stab knife is held in a dagger-type grip and is used for making two perpendicular cuts, the chip being removed by a third cut from the chip knife. Locate the knife point on the line where the cut will be deepest, then push it down and "roll" it along the line, to give a cut that graduates from deep to shallow. Repeat the action in a second cut, at about 90° to the first, so that the deep parts are adjacent. Then take out the chip with the chip knife.

Practice your technique on some scrap wood before beginning the project. Keep the knife at an angle of about 60°: any steeper makes the cut too deep and difficult to do; any shallower means the carving will look flat and lifeless. For the deeper cuts in the project pattern, you will need to remove a small chip from the center of the shape first to reduce pressure on the knife for the finishing cuts.

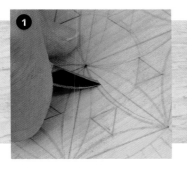

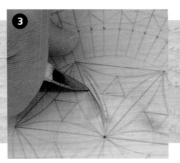

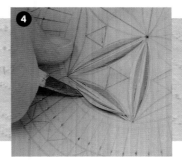

Stage one

1 Begin with the deep-cut petal shapes. Hold the wood in your free hand, and make the initial "relieving" cut to remove a small sliver before taking out the full-size chip.

2 Turn the workpiece to enable you to continue carving in the same direction as you make the second cut. The chip should pop out.
3 Make the first finishing cut close to the line.

4 Carve the second finishing cut to the line and release the chip. Clear any remaining whiskers of wood from the valley bottom with some gentle tidying cuts. You have now reached the point illustrated right. The five remaining similar sections would normally be carved in sequence at this stage.

First stage

The outer edges of one petal have been completed.

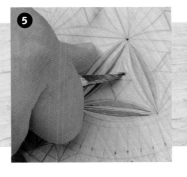

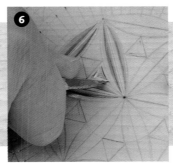

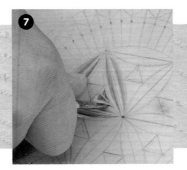

Stage two

5 Three knife cuts are made to release this triangular chip. Again, remove a small chip from the middle first to ease the final cuts. Notice how the wood is rotated in the hand to present the line to be cut. This

ensures that consistency of depth and angle of blade are maintained.
6 Beginning the second series of cuts up to the line to give the finished shape.

7 At the completion of the three cuts, the chip is released. The petal section of your carving will now appear as shown right.

Second stage

The petal is almost complete, with the exception of the central triangle.

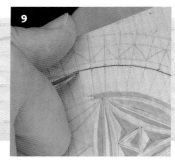

Stage three

8 Carve the central triangles by the same method, taking out a small "pressure chip" and then making the three final cuts. You have now brought the section to the point illustrated right. Again, the other five would usually be finished to the same degree before proceeding to the next stage.

Third stage

The petal is now complete.

Stage four

9 The circular groove is a long V-shaped chip. This is a shallow cut, so no pressure chip needs to be removed. In chip carving, always try to make your initial cuts away from previous carving to reduce the risk of raised parts of the pattern flaking off, especially on

end grain. Here, the inner V has been carved and the first cut of the outer V is being made.

10 The chip comes out cleanly as the second cut is made on the outer V. Your carving will now appear as shown below left, with the two V cuts in place. You should complete each circle before continuing.

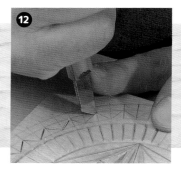

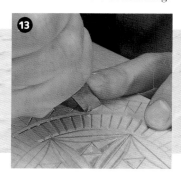

Fourth stage

Both circles have been started. They should be completed before you move to the next stage.

Stage five

11 Carve the radiating dovetail shapes with shorter V cuts. Turn the wood for the second cut, which removes the chip.

12 Stab cuts are used to set in the outer ring of "dragon's teeth," and the chip is released by a third cut from the chip knife. Set in two cuts, at about 90° to each other, with the stab knife held like a dagger. Position the point and push.

13 When the desired depth is reached, the knife blade is lowered forward along the line to its junction with the next line. This gives a cut which slopes gradually from nothing to the full depth at the corner. Practice on some scrap wood.

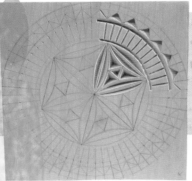

14 When two stab cuts are complete, remove the chip using a chip knife. If the chip is too large to come out conveniently in one cut, take out a small chip first. Here the second cut is being made, close to the line, to release the remainder of the chip. This section of the pattern will now have reached the point illustrated right with the dovetail pattern and "dragon's teeth" carved. Again, the circles of both should be completed.

15 Sand the work or use an eraser to remove pencil marks.

Finishes

The finished piece was painted with satin polyurethane varnish, rubbed with steel wool, and waxed.

Fifth stage

In order to demonstrate all the different cuts, one segment has been finished ahead of the others. When carving this yourself, it is better to complete each type of cut all around the circle, before moving on to the next.

Coffee-pot stand

Peter Clothier

———

Chip carving is particularly suited to decorating furniture and other domestic objects.

4

· · · · · · · · · · · · · · · O B J E C T I V E · · · · · · · · · · · · · · ·

To carve a simple design with a clean, flat, recessed background, suitable for a box or lamp base.

BOX OR TABLE LAMP

Charity collection boxes are all too often unimaginatively shaped and made of dull plastic. A wooden box is more pleasing and may attract more contributions, as well as being fun to make. If you do not want a collecting box, leave out the coin slot and use the box for storing small items. Most people love wooden boxes, whether they have a practical purpose or not.

The shape would also make a good table lamp. Cut out the center or the whole of the beam and attach a lamp fixture to the lid. Holes can easily be drilled in the top and the bottom for the cord, if necessary. A lamp base will need some ballast, so insert a small plastic bag of sand before attaching the lid.

DESIGN CONSIDERATIONS

I once contributed to an auction of hand-made collection boxes, and the huge variety of shapes and sizes on display demonstrated that ideas for this object are limitless. I therefore began this project by thinking about my priorities: a simple construction on a household scale. The design would need to be interesting but unfussy.

The chosen pattern is based upon the blind arcading on a 10th-century church tower at Barton on Humber in eastern England. There is similar decoration on other early churches in England. This so-called "long and short" work was usually made either by attaching the stones at the time of building or by putting stones into an existing wall, but there is one small church dating from the seventh or very early eighth century, at Bradford on Avon in Wiltshire, on which arcading like this was achieved in the tenth century by carving the recessed parts in the existing ashlar walls. The thin uprights are reminiscent of wooden structures, and one theory suggests that when the Anglo-Saxons started to build in stone, they retained the familiar look of the half-timbered buildings that they were replacing.

My aim was not to make the box look like a church tower, but to

TOOLS AND MATERIALS

- Basic toolkit
- Craft or chip carving knife
- Steel straightedge
- Small back saw such as a tenon saw
- Marking or cutting gauge
- Try square
- Small hammer
- Block plane
- Drills — ¼ in and ³⁄₁₆ in
- Plough plane (optional)
- Hand router (optional)
- Awl
- White woodworking glue
- Basswood (or virtually any soft- or hardwood)
- Useful power tools if available: electric drill and router

adapt the pattern to fit the box. The lid has no particular historical links, but if you want people to put money in your box, they have to notice it and it should intrigue them. The bar and the brackets which form the hinge and locking device were designed to draw the eye while remaining in keeping with the architectural quality of the piece.

The box is constructed so that the two side panels fit into channels in the backs of the other two. This serves a dual purpose, giving the impression of buttresses at the corners and hiding the joint itself. The latter will be glued and pegged for strength. The bottom of the box also fits into channels, helping to keep the structure square and providing a safe floor for coins. The slight tapering of the sides toward the top is just a whim. You will need to make accurate measured drawings of the fronts and backs of two panels, the top and bottom of the lid (which should also be shown in elevation), and a bracket in elevation.

CUTTING LIST

PLANED BASSWOOD	inches		inches		inches	Quantity
Side panels	7½	×	4½	×	⅝	2
Side panels	7½	×	3¾	×	⅝	2 *
Top	5½	×	4½	×	⅝	1
Bottom	3⅝	×	3⅜	×	⅝	1
Bar	7½	×	⅝	×	⅝	1 *
Brackets	2½	×	1	×	⅝	4

Also a few odd pieces made from scraps.
*I bought 4½ inches wood and cut the rod from one of the narrow side panels.

HARDWOOD DOWEL ROD	inches		inches diameter	Quantity
Hinge pin	3	×	¼	1
Bolt	3	×	¼	1
Pegs	1	×	¼	24

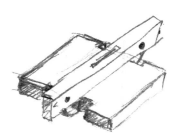

PLANS

Draw these plans and elevations carefully to actual size to get a clear picture of the parts. Drawing it on paper first is a very useful rehearsal for drawing it on the wood.

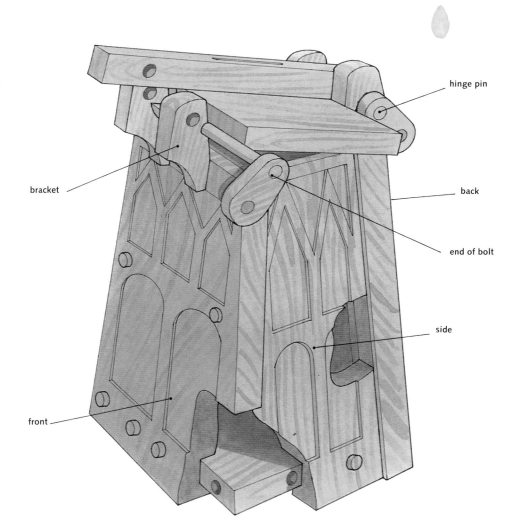

Locking device

One side of the bracket holds the hinge pin and the other side the bolt. The lid is attached permanently at the hinge end.

bracket

front

hinge pin

back

end of bolt

side

Side assembly

This cutaway diagram shows how the base and sides slot together into the channels. Make sure that everything is square before you glue it.

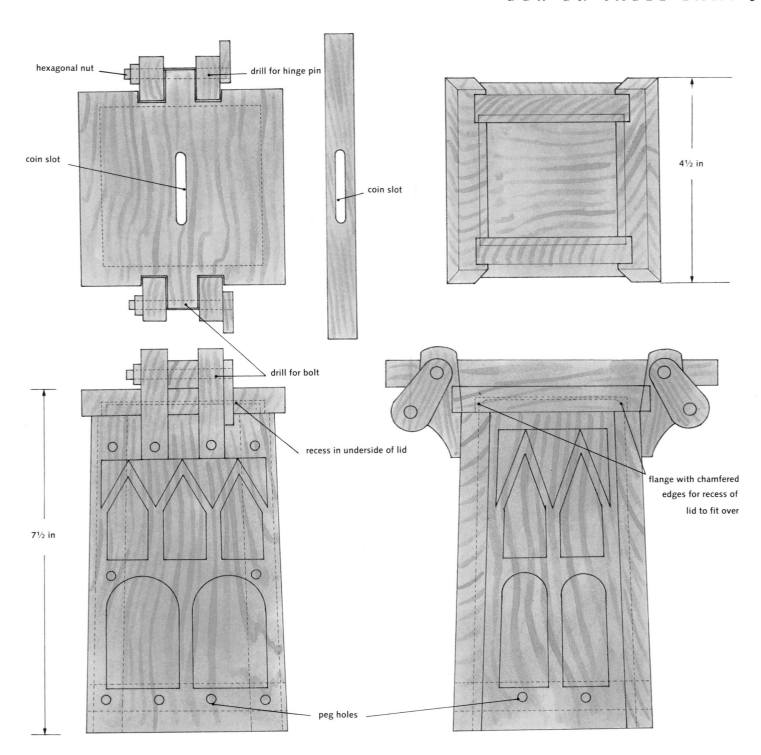

hexagonal nut

drill for hinge pin

coin slot

coin slot

4½ in

drill for bolt

recess in underside of lid

flange with chamfered
edges for recess of
lid to fit over

7½ in

peg holes

METHOD

The aim in this project is to carve a flat design as cleanly as possible. In effect you will be leaving the surface much as you did in the trial cuts (p. 42) and the woodcut (p. 74) and making a sunken, or recessed, surface which will be as flat as you can make it. Some of the work can be done with straight chisels, but there will also be useful practice with grounding tools. The panels will be carved before the box is assembled.

Stage one

① Draw all the details on the fronts and the backs of the panels before shaping them, because, while they are rectangular, you can use a try square for the cross lines. If your wood for all the panels is the same width, as mine was (see cutting list on page 95), draw the narrow panel details close to one edge, and saw off the scrap wood from one of them to make the bar for the lid.

② Shade in, or hatch, the areas to be carved out and plane the sides so that they taper toward the top. You have now reached the point illustrated right, showing a broad panel.

Stage two

③ Next mark the grooves in the backs of the panels into which the sides and bottom will fit. Score the lines carefully several times with a marking or cutting gauge, starting with the point just touching the wood and gradually changing the angle to cut more deeply with each stroke you make.

④ When working across the grain, you will find it more satisfactory to mark the line with a craft or chip carving knife against a steel straightedge. You may prefer to use a knife for much of your other marking, too, but again, score the line gently to begin with, and be sure to keep firm pressure on the straightedge, holding the knife close to the steel. This is especially important when cutting along the grain of the wood, because the knife

has a tendency to follow the grain instead of the straightedge. Draw the knife along the line repeatedly to increase its depth. If using the knife along the grain on the wide panels, it is safer to cut with the

straightedge on the outside; a deviating blade will dig into the groove. When cutting the lines near the outer edges, place another panel alongside to provide enough surface for the straightedge to rest on.

First stage

The working lines have been drawn on. Shaded areas indicate waste wood.

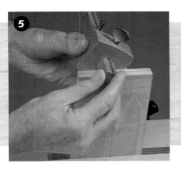

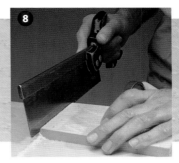

5 Mark the lines for the rabbet to hold the lid at the top of the panel fronts. It is easier to use a marking gauge on the end grain than to balance a straightedge and knife. Work in from each end of the line and, as before, have the point or blade at an angle so that

the first stroke scores lightly and subsequent strokes bite more deeply.

6 Use a try square and knife to mark across the ends of the rabbet on the broad panels. These coincide with the inner edges of the grooves on the back.

7 and **8** Score across the front of the panel, and cut down to the line with a tenon saw.

9 and **10** Using a chisel, carve in from the end, above the line, toward the saw cut, to remove most of the waste. Then take off thin shavings across the grain to clean up. When carving across the grain, stop before you reach the far side and cut back in the other

direction to avoid splitting off a piece unintentionally. In the case of basswood, it is not difficult to carve across with a series of firm knife cuts interspersed with removing the waste, instead of just using a tenon saw.

11 Turn the wood over and carve out the channels on the back. The process is similar to making the rabbet (see p. 45). Use a chip carving knife and a chisel, or if the wood is too hard for a knife, cut the sides of the groove with a chisel and

mallet. If you have a hand router or a plough plane, you can take the grooves out with that. For the hand router, the sides of the grooves must be pre-cut, and for the plough plane, they should be well marked with a knife.

12 Remove the waste with a chisel when cutting across the grain. With all the channels on the broad panels complete, do the same to the narrow panels which have only a horizontal groove for the bottom to slide into.

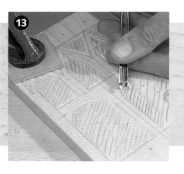
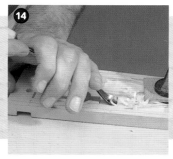
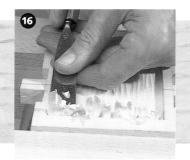

Stage three

13 To carve the pattern, start by following around inside the lines with a V tool. Then use a very sharp blade, such as a chip carving knife and a straightedge, to score once lightly along the lines then with more pressure. Use the knife on the waste side of the line and examine the grain carefully before deciding which way to draw the knife. For example, in the "V's" at the top, cut from the inside angles toward the springing line, and then the opposite way from the outside angles toward the apexes on the outside of the arches. You have to cut the curved tops of the round arches freehand. Work away from the center of the top of each arch down to the springing lines at the sides. If your wood is too hard for a knife to be used easily, make the cuts down vertically with chisels and gouges, using a mallet if necessary.

14 Carve away the wood which is not wanted in the pattern. One way to do this is to re-move the bulk of the wood by carving a series of grooves across the grain with a No. 8 or 9 gouge, and then using a flatter bent gouge to take it all down to a relatively even sur-face. Cut along the edges again with knife or chisel, using a straightedge if necessary, and work with a bent chisel and corner chisels to clean up the surface and take the pieces out of the corners. To remove the wood in the acute angles of the triangular arches, cut sharply down the sides right into the corners with a slim corner chisel or sharp knife, then come in as flatly and as far as possible with your smal-lest chisel before flicking up-ward; this will usually take the thin wedge out quite neatly. Your aim is to make recesses of even depth, with reasonably, but not mechanically, smooth surfaces, and clean-cut edges.

The lid

15 The lid is basically 4½ inches square with small pro-jections, like corbels, which fit under the bar. Saw in from each side along the line as far as the bar lines, then saw both sides of – and just outside – the bar lines as far as the inner corners of the recesses, which will hold the brackets when the lid is closed. Make short saw cuts into the outer corners of these recesses. Remove the wood from the recesses in be-tween the saw cuts with a chisel; work from both the top and the bottom.

16 The lid is recessed on the underside to fit over the tops of the side panels and sit on the rabbets. This recess is deeper than the pattern but carved in exactly the same way, and the surface can be left more uneven. (You might like to do this before the side panels to give yourself some practice on a part which is not normally seen.) The projec-tions in the middles of the two sides can now be carved to make quadrant-shaped corbels

to go under each end of the bar. This is best done with a chisel slicing around from each side, as well as following the curve over the middle.

17 and **18** Mark the centers of the peg holes with a pointed tool or awl to prevent the drill bit from wandering, and drill all the holes for the pegs with a ¼ inch drillbit.

19 Before attaching the bar to the lid, make the coin slot. Draw the center line down the entire length of the bar, top and bottom. In the middle of the top and bottom, draw two parallel lines 1¾ inches long and ⅛ inch from the center line on each side, joining the ends perpendicularly to it. On the center line, ⅛ inch in from each end of the coin slot, mark with a pointed tool or awl the position for two holes, and drill straight through. Score the lines between the holes with a craft knife. Then mark and drill as many ¼ inch holes in between as you can.

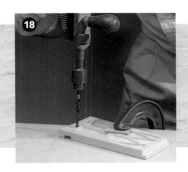

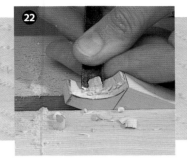

20 Gradually clean out the slot with a chisel, working from both sides as before to avoid splitting pieces off. Mark the position of the slot on the top of the lid and drill and clean it out in the same way. On the underside of the lid, about halfway between the ends of the slot and the edges of the recess, and on the center line, drill ³⁄₁₆ inch holes and countersink them.

21 Clamp the bar in position on the top of the lid, make starter holes for the screws and put the screws in. This is not a permanent attachment, so do not glue it yet. Tidy up the coin slot so that it is continuous right through the lid and bar. The corbels under the bar ends can also be shaved to make uniform surfaces with the bar's sides.

22 Carve the concave curves on the undersides of the brackets. First remove a wedge with a mallet and chisel, working with the grain. Do this in stages to follow a line which runs from the top to the bottom of the curve; then carve in from each side across the grain to make the curve. Once again, do not try to gouge off too much in one cut.

23 Shave off the sloping inner side of each bracket. To round off the tops of the brackets you can hold them all together in a vice and carve in from either side to make the curves. Then give a slight chamfer to the edges of the curves individually. Take the two broad side panels and, in the spaces indicated for the brackets, make marks with a pointed tool about halfway between the peg holes and the edge of the rabbet above, and drill ³⁄₁₆ inch holes for screws. Hold each bracket in position individually, mark through the hole from behind, make a starter hole with a pointed tool, and put in a screw; make

sure the bracket is positioned correctly and tighten the screw. When all four are securely in place, drill through the existing peg holes from behind, with a ¼ inch drillbit to extend the peg holes through the brackets. Check the position of each bracket again before drilling, and if possible hold it in a vice. With all the brackets screwed, tap dowels temporarily into place through the peg holes.

Preassembly

24 Assemble the box with the lid in position and hold together with clamps. Using a pointed tool, mark on one bracket the position of the hole for the hinge pin, and on another the hole for the bolt. With the whole piece level and steady, drill both holes with a ¼ inch drillbit right through brackets and beam. Drill the bolt hole again with a ¼ inch clearance drillbit. Push the hinge pin through and test the lid to see if it will open and close. The channels for the brackets will almost

certainly need adjustment, and the recess under the lid may also need attention.

25 The hinge pin and bolt are identical, each consisting of a 2¾ inch length of ¼ inch dowel rod. A piece has to be glued to one end which, in the case of the bolt, will serve as a grip. I have used a slightly wedge-shaped piece of wood rounded at the ends and with two ¼ inch holes drilled in it ⁵⁄₈ inch apart. The wood measures 1¼ × ⁵⁄₈ × ¼ inch. Glue the pieces of dowel into the hole at the narrower end. At the other ends, attach octagonal or hexagonal "nuts" measuring about ½ inch across the flat sides. Make these by drilling ¼ inch holes in a scrap and squaring the wood around the hole. Shape the facets by removing the corners with a sharp chisel. The thickness should be about ¼ inch.

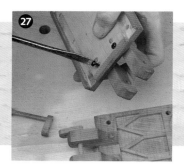

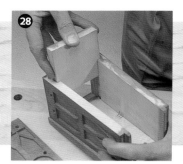

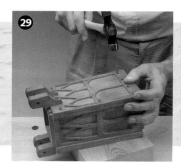

26 If you want to stain your box, do that next, but before dismantling it, mark the lid, the bar and the box itself at the hinge end; identify each bracket, and its position, as you remove it – say, by numbering from 1 to 4 – because all must return to the same places. Put all the parts on several layers of newspaper, and equip yourself with an apron and rubber gloves. Before staining the box, make a test on a scrap and let it dry. If the color is acceptable, brush it onto all the carved parts and use a rag to apply it to smooth areas. Apply the stain around the edges and on the ends. The side panels should be stained on the back as far up as the horizontal grooves. The underside of the bottom is stained, and the lid should be stained all over. The short dowels for the pegs need only have one end dipped, but the hinge pin and the bolt can be stained completely. Your box has now reached the end of Stage Three, as illustrated by the narrow panel right.

Third stage

Stain the finished parts before assembling the box.

Stage four

27 When the stain is dry, assemble the parts. This time, use white woodworking glue on the brackets and dowels, and fasten the screws tightly.

28 Put glue in the channels and push the narrow sides down into them. Do the same for the bottom, sliding it into position before attaching the fourth panel. Make sure that everything is square, and clamp it while it dries. Glue the bar onto the lid and screw it from the underside. When putting in screws, always screw down onto a firm surface if possible. It is important to be sure that the screwdriver cannot damage you if it slips.

29 Pegs other than the bracket pegs must be inserted after the glue has set. Drill all the peg holes to a depth of about $5/8$ inch, but check carefully that you can do this without piercing the carved pattern. The top holes outside the brackets are the most likely to have insufficient wood behind them. The dowels can easily be shortened. Reduce them to

between ⅝ inch and ¾ inch, put a little white glue into the holes, rest the box on a firm surface, and tap the dowels in.

30 The nut for the bolt has to be attached permanently on the bracket, so push the bolt through, apply a little glue to one side of the nut, and slide it along the bolt until it is pressing against the bracket. Drill a tiny hole – say, ⅟₁₆ inch – through the nut, and tap a brad through the nut into the bracket. Withdraw the bolt, wipe off any glue, and leave the box until all the glue has dried.

Before attaching the lid permanently at the hinge end, oil the box and lid separately with Danish oil. When they are thoroughly dry, position the lid, put some glue on the big end of the hinge pin, and push it through until it is pressing against the side of the bracket. Then apply some glue to the nut and slide that along in the same way at the other end.

Finishing

Finishing is always a matter of personal taste. A painted or shiny coating did not seem right for this box, but the wood was somewhat dull for a colorless finish. Instead it was enriched with an application of pitch pine alcohol stain, followed by three coats of Danish oil, so that all it needs is an occasional rub with a little wax polish. Stains usually fade, but as the wood matures at the same time, the processes are complementary and the end result is attractive. Staining must be done before the box is assembled, because stain is repelled by white glue.

Charity box
Antony Denning

———

The simple design and warm finish of this box would be equally appealing as a lamp base.

. . . . OBJECTIVE . . . .

To become familiar with letter-cutting techniques by designing and carving a variety of letters. The results should be well designed and easy to read.

LETTER CUTTING

The basic process of carving letters in wood is extremely simple; the skill lies in doing it well. The key to good lettering lies as much in the spaces between the letters as in the letters themselves. A group of letters imperfectly cut but well arranged looks better than beautiful letters badly spaced. This is another example of the balance between art and craft, because spacing depends on the eye and not on rules.

The Romans, who were renowned for their carved inscriptions, tended to space their letters farther apart than we do today. This is probably because the printed word has accustomed us to reading a group of letters rapidly as a unit. Printing has made it difficult for us to look at spacing critically. The structure of letterpress type made it impossible to arrange the spaces between letters by eye, which means we have become used to bad spacing.

Letters can be either incised – cut into the surface – or raised, when the surface around them is carved away. Incised letters are more common, probably because they can be cut more finely, especially when

they have serifs, and also because there is additional work in chiseling away the background for raised letters.

DESIGN CONSIDERATIONS

We use the Roman alphabet and Arabic numerals, but the principles governing the design of a piece of lettering remain the same whatever its cultural origins. Because we take in words as units, it is the shape of the entire unit – or the spacing and arrangement of several units – which is important.

It is advisable to use capital letters only until you have acquired a fair degree of skill and confidence. To draw and space the letters correctly all at once is difficult, so try starting with the following system. Choose a one-word inscription, such as the name of your house, and determine the shape of letters you want. Use the alphabet illustrated, or look for alternative letter forms in a catalogue of type faces. Decide the height of the letters, and draw a set of parallel lines that distance apart on a sheet of paper.

TOOLS AND MATERIALS

- Three straight chisels: No. 1, 20 mm, 13 mm, and 6 mm (¾ in, ½ in and ¼ in)
- Skew chisel No. 2 10 mm (⅜ in)
- Three straight gouges: Nos. 3, 4, and 6, all 6 mm (¼ in)
- Black carbon paper
- Any hardwood with an even grain and color
- Useful power tools if available: none

Draw each letter individually until you are satisfied with it. You will find it helpful to draw in a few faint guide lines to make your letters consistent – say, one at the halfway mark, and others the width of the top and bottom horizontals of an E – but do not be slavish in keeping to these. Occasional lightly ruled verticals will provide a reference for correct vertical strokes.

Make yourself a ruler on a piece of paper or thin poster board, marking on it the full width and three-quarter, half and quarter widths of the vertical strokes. You could decide, for instance, to make the full width of the vertical strokes one-eighth of the height of the letter. Once that is established and drawn on your rule, it only takes a second to check the widths of your full-width verticals, and so on.

When drawing an O, take it a hair's breadth over the line above and below. Allow the points at the base of M, N, V, and W just to pierce the bottom line, and those at the tops of A and W similarly to penetrate the top line. When all the letters are drawn to your satisfaction, cut the containing rectangle around each one. Draw a new pair of parallel lines on a fresh sheet of paper and arrange the letters between them until the spacing looks right. You may want to adjust some letter shapes to make them fit better with their neighbors. (For example, an R next to a T could have a longer tail than one next to an A.) Then glue the letters down.

Now pin the design on the wall and look critically again at the spacing. Turn the paper upside down and take a further look. Ask yourself if the letters make a well-balanced unit. When the design is upright, can you read the word easily? If it is incorrectly spaced, there may appear to be a break in it. If you are not satisfied and feel that slight alterations are needed, draw parallel lines on some tracing paper

RAISED LETTERS

This illustrates the difference between incised and raised letters. To carve letters in relief, the wood around them has to be removed to an even depth. It is usual to leave a slight slope on the sides to give strength to letters which would otherwise be vulnerable, especially at the ends.

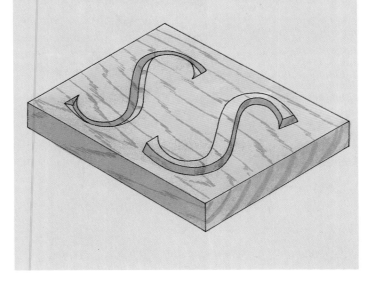

and trace the design, adjusting the spaces as necessary. It does not matter if these tracings are not as perfectly drawn as the original because you can go back to your best letters when required. It is a good idea to shade in the letters because this gives a clearer picture of the effect. The adjustment of spacing is a subtle and important process, so it is worth taking time over it. If you leave your design for a night, or even for a week, and return to it with a fresh eye, you will be able to see it more clearly.

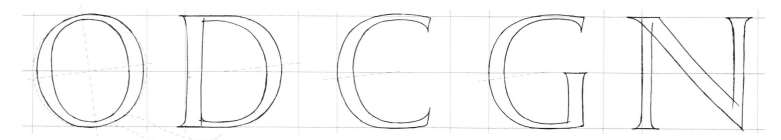

Letters

O (Q) All letters should be designed in relation to O, which is not quite circular in outline. The thinnest part is about ⅓ of a wide stroke.

D (I) The vertical wide stem forms the letter I. Its sides are neither straight nor parallel, but curve slightly inward.

C and **G** are related to the left-hand half of O. The tops and bottoms of each letter are only slightly curved. The vertical stem of G is a full wide stroke and reaches up to the center line.

N The vertical stems should be ⅔ of a wide stroke. The diagonal, a full wide stroke, is slightly curved.

H The crossbar is half a wide stroke in thickness and rests on the center line.

A The left-hand oblique stroke is ⅔

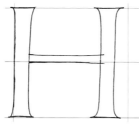

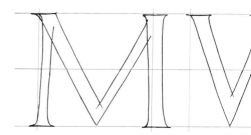

of a wide stroke in thickness, while the crossbar is ½ a wide stroke.

V The same width as A, but the diagonals are slightly curved.

U The same width as A and V; the right-hand stem is ⅔ of a wide stroke in thickness. Start the curve low down.

T The crossbar is ½ a wide stroke in thickness. The width of T is variable to achieve even spacing and texture.

M Slightly wider than a square. The two outer strokes are slightly diagonal, and the inner strokes are slightly curved.

W Not a double V. All four strokes are slightly curved, narrow ones ⅔ of a wide stroke in thickness. As in M, the triangular spaces at each side should be similar.

X fits into ¾ of a square. The top of the letter is narrower, and asymmetry is generated by difference in stroke width.

Z The main diagonal has a slight curve; horizontals are ½ a wide stroke in thickness.

Y The junction sits on the center line. The right-hand diagonal is ⅔ of a wide stroke in thickness.

J The only letter which breaks out of the parallel lines. It can be difficult to use, but the shape of the tail can be changed.

E Related to ½ a square, its horizontals are ½ a wide stroke in thickness, and are of slightly different lengths.

F Note that the central horizontal is slightly lower than that in E.

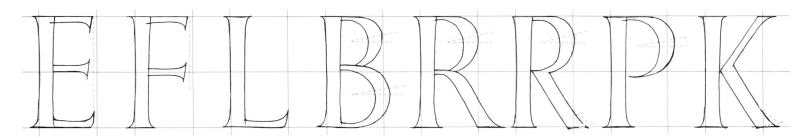

L *The horizontal is slightly longer than that of E.*
B *Each bow has its widest point above the center of the*

curve. The enclosed shapes give the letter much of its character and quality.
R *The bow is half the height of the*

letter. The angle of the tail is variable to make even spacing easier.
R *This version harmonizes better*

with K, and many find it easier to carve. Lifting the foot gives R a gentle forward movement.
P *The upper bow is*

deeper and wider than that of R and B, and its counter has a subtly different shape.
K *The proportions*

relate to those of R. The upper diagonal is 2/3 of a wide stroke in thickness and so relates to the corresponding stroke

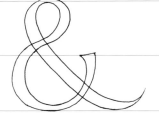

in Y.
S *is built up from two unequal circles, the upper one being the smaller, placed so that they lean forward very slightly.*

& *Built up from two circles like numeral 8, but with the upper circle much the smaller. The curved diagonal is a full wide stroke.*

Numerals
1 *Like I, but with the top modified.*
2 *The top and its serif relate to C, but in reverse; horizontal is 1/2 wide stroke in*

thickness with serif related to L.
3 *Horizontal 1/2 wide stroke in thickness, with serif related to T. Bottom serif related to S.*

4 *Diagonal 2/3 of a wide stroke in thickness; horizontal 1/2 a wide stroke with serif related to T.*
5 *Proportions similar to those of 3.*

0 *Much narrower than letter O, and symmetrical.*
6 *Left-hand side related to O; proportion of bow related to 5; serif*

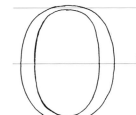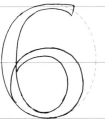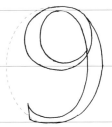

related to C.
9 *Related to O, but not an upside-down 6; the bow is much smaller.*
7 *Horizontal 1/2 a*

wide stroke in width, with serif related to T. Placement of the bottom serif in relation to the top one is critical.

8 *Built up from two circles like S, but without the forward lean. Note differences in thickness between*

the two sides of each bow.

DRAWING A LETTER

To transfer your drawing to the wood, first draw lines on the wood. Tape the paper to the wood with the black carbon paper underneath. Make sure that the lines on the paper align perfectly with those on the wood. Tape your drawing to the wood with masking tape. Draw lightly over your drawing with a ballpoint pen. Check each letter as you do it to make sure that the transfer is working. When all the letters are traced, you will see that the outlines look shaky. Make minor corrections with a very soft pencil.

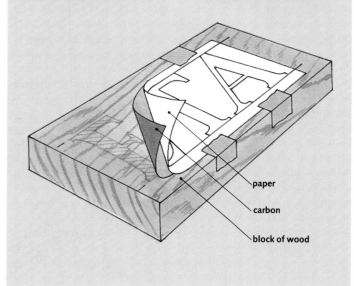

paper

carbon

block of wood

METHOD

This project uses incised lettering and incorporates all the techniques you will need to carve any letter of the alphabet. There are two basic incising methods known as chasing and stabbing. In chasing, the V section is carved with a skew chisel with an angle about 75° back from the point, starting with a V which is narrower than the final letter and gradually enlarging it by the removal of fine shavings from alternate sides, following the line of the letter. In stabbing, a combination of chisels and gouges is used to form the letters, and the tools are driven in at an angle to form the V section. Many carvers stab vertically down the center of the letter before making angled cuts from each side. Most letter cutters develop their own methods, which are often a blend of the two techniques. Here the carver uses a stabbing technique, with chasing to finish some letters. He sharpens his tools with long bevels and slightly curved edges. Not all letter cutters do this, but it is obviously worth trying methods which get excellent results. If you expect to do a lot of letter cutting, it is a good idea to keep some chisels and gouges specially for the purpose.

If you would like to carve raised letters, use an alphabet in which there are no very thin strokes or fine serifs. Draw the letters on the wood and cut away the spaces between them in the same way as you carved the background of the pattern on the box (p. 94). Leave a slight slope on the edges of the letters, because if you cut them perpendicular to the surface, they tend to be rather fragile.

It is possible to cut letters in any wood, but hardwoods with a close grain and an even color are the best choice. If the grain or figure is too apparent, it makes the letters difficult to read.

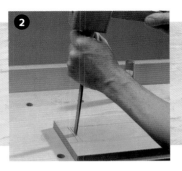

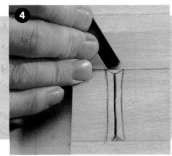

Letter I

1 After drawing, score lightly down the center with a chisel. The stem is called a wide stroke.

2 Using a 13 mm (½ in) No. 1 chisel, make a stab cut to the full depth of the letter. Carve to within half a wide stroke of the top and base – not right to the ends.

3 Make Y-shaped sloping cuts to the corners at the ends of the stem with a No. 2 skew chisel.

4 Still using the No. 2 chisel, cut the sloping "triangles" of wood from each end of the stem.

5 The bulk of the wood is removed by downward sloping cuts, starting and ending a little short of the ends of the stem. Note how each cut overlaps the previous one so that a smooth, slightly curved surface is produced. Use a wide 20 mm (¾ in) No. 1 chisel.

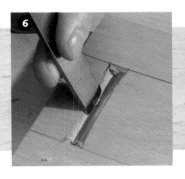

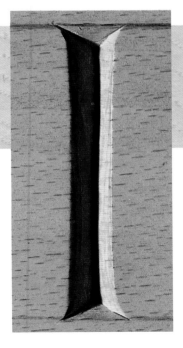

6 Use the same wide chisel without the mallet to pare away any irregularities. Notice how the edge is controlled by the fingers.

7 Finish the stem by cutting away the small triangles of wood left at the ends. Make sure that the sides run smoothly out to the corners.

Letter I
The completed letter.

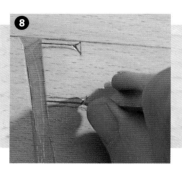

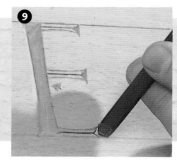

Letter E

8 Start the E by carving a wide stem as before. Then stab in the horizontal arms. Remember they are narrower, and therefore less deep, than the main stem. Also they run along the grain, so the stab cuts must be made gently. Add little Y-shaped cuts into the corners at the end of each arm.

9 Cut out the end of each arm with a No. 2 skew chisel.

10 Using downward sloping cuts, gently carve out the wood from the arms. Often a sideways slicing cut is better than trying to cut straight down. Control the blade with your fingers.

11 Smooth and finish off the arms with chasing cuts, pushing the chisel along the line of cut. Care is needed here to make sure that the cut does not run out along the grain. If it begins to do so, stop at once and carve in the reverse direction.

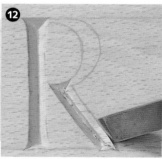

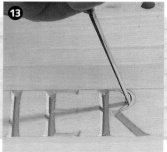

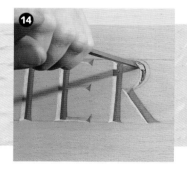

Letter E
The completed letter.

Letter R

12 Carve the wide upright stem. Then stab cut the tail and carve the triangles at either end. Cut away the wood from the left side of the tail first, carving downward to avoid splitting.

13 Using a No. 3 or No. 4 gouge (depending on the tightness of the curve), stab in the rounded part of the R, known as the bowl. The gouge is held off the vertical at the start of the cut; when the cut is finished, it should be upright.

14 Carve the inside of the bowl with a 6 mm (¼ in) chisel. Start at the junction with the tail and cut up and around to the middle. Then carve from the top of the stem around to the middle again. Overlap the cuts for a smooth surface.

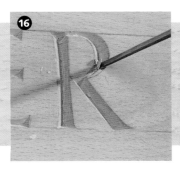

15 Use a No. 3 or No. 4 gouge to cut the outside of the bowl. Begin in the middle (at the deepest part), cutting up and around to the top of the stem.

16 Return to the middle and cut around and down to the junction with the tail. The gouge will probably leave a "scalloped" surface where the main cuts are made. This should be smoothed by delicate paring away of the ridges.

Letter R
The completed letter.

Letter G
17 Stab the entire letter G before carving the upright wide stem. Remove the triangle of wood from the top end of the bowl.

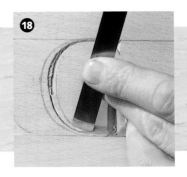

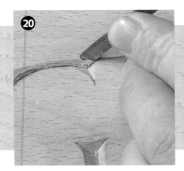

18 Using 13 mm (½ in) and 6 mm (¼ in) No. 1 chisels, cut the inside of the bowl, starting at either end and working toward the middle.

19 Cut the outside of the bowl with a No. 3 gouge. The "scallops" produced by the gouge will later be smoothed by paring.

20 When most of the outside of the bowl has been roughly cut, carve the top of the G from the end leftward to the start of the curve. This has to be done delicately with a No. 3 gouge. The ridges can then be pared away to finish the letter.

Letter G
The completed letter.

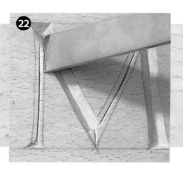
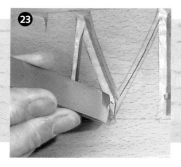
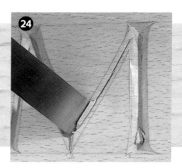

Letter M

21 Begin by stabbing the whole letter. Be especially careful at the acute angle junctions; stab them as gently as possible.

22 Cut both wide stems, but stop a little short of the V-junction in the middle. Then carve the right side of the nar-row left-hand stroke. Begin at the junction, using a wide chisel and making sure that it overlaps the junction completely to achieve a clean cut.

23 When the left-hand narrow stroke is complete, cut the left side of the central V-junction with the same chisel.

24 Begin the left side of the angled narrow stroke at its bottom junction. Again make sure that the chisel completely covers the junction.

25 Finish the letter by cutting away the right-hand side of the central V-junction.

26 The completed letter M. Notice particularly the forms of the acute-angled junctions.

Letter M

The completed letter.

Letter S

27 Stab the whole letter, including the Y-cuts at the ends.

28 Carve the inside curves by starting at their outermost points. Make the short cuts outward to the corners, then work inward and around each curve. Stop when the chisel is cutting across the grain.

29 Begin cutting the outside curves across the grain and work inward toward the central part of the letter.

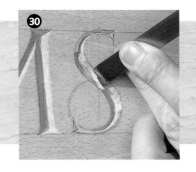

30 As you reach the straight central part, change from a gouge to a straight chisel. Continue along the center portion to join the inside curve cut earlier.

31 Cut away the triangles of wood at the two ends.

32 Carve the remaining outside curves, beginning across the grain and working outward to the top and bottom of each curve. Finally, cut leftward from the top corner, and rightward from the bottom corner, to form the narrow parts of the letter and so complete it.

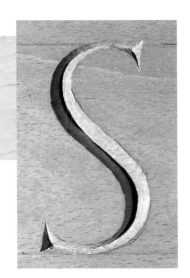

Finishing

For signwork to be read easily outdoors, it is usually necessary to paint the letters. For interior work, however, painting or gilding can diminish their three-dimensional quality. Simply treating the wood with oil and shellac or varnish – depending on how much exposure the letters will have – can be more effective.

Letter S
The completed letter.

Bread platter
Martin Wenham

*This cherry platter
has been given an
olive oil finish.*

. . . . **OBJECTIVE** . . . .

To carve a pleasing functional object with a smooth transition from bowl to handle and a harmonious overall shape.

SPOONS AND SALAD UTENSILS

Wooden spoons and salad utensils may sound mundane, but they have interesting aspects for the carver and can be highly enjoyable to carve. They are fully three-dimensional, so they will be viewed from different angles, and they need to be visually attractive, tactile, and practical for their purposes.

DESIGN CONSIDERATIONS

It is probably difficult to think about such familiar objects with a fresh and open mind. Spoons and salad utensils have been around for so long that it seems likely that the perfect shape has already been achieved. Look at as many examples as you can, with a constructively critical eye. You will notice that most are not hand-carved; so perhaps that is a good starting point? What are the best shapes for carving that will also be functional? If you visualize yourself serving salad, it is obvious that two implements are more satisfactory than one. You might want to scoop up dressing with one utensil, so you can

make that spoon-shaped, but the other server will only be used to hold the salad against the spoon. It does not need long prongs, nor does it have to imitate a metal fork. It might not resemble a fork at all; but it must, of course, match the spoon.

In my case, there was an additional consideration because the salad utensils had to be carved from a single, rather narrow, piece of wood, and that necessitated an asymmetrical design.

It is a good idea to make some rough sketches of the shapes which come to mind, and examine them critically from the visual and the practical points of view. When your designs seem right, decide upon the dimensions of your utensils, and carefully draw plan shapes, actual size. Then draw the elevations. In my case the plan shapes are the same, though one will be reversed, and the elevations are similar, but obviously the fork end can be much thinner than the bowl of the spoon. Templates are useful for redrawing the shapes on the wood every time the lines are carved off; I like to have one traced from the plan and one from the

TOOLS AND MATERIALS
- Basic toolkit
- Coping saw
- Cabinet scrapers
- Spokeshave
- Small drill bit (for hole in spoon handle)
- Any non-toxic hardwood
- Useful power tools if available: band saw or jig saw, and electric drill

elevation. Templates can be cut from tracing paper, but thick construction paper or thin posterboard are firmer.

A similar approach applies to spoons. Think of the purposes for which wooden spoons are used, such as scraping bowls and saucepans, stirring and sampling, and even for crushing garlic, perhaps? Any or all of these considerations may influence your design.

PLANS

Square up some strong cartridge paper and transfer the plans and elevations (including the construction and center lines) to make templates (see pp. 19–20).

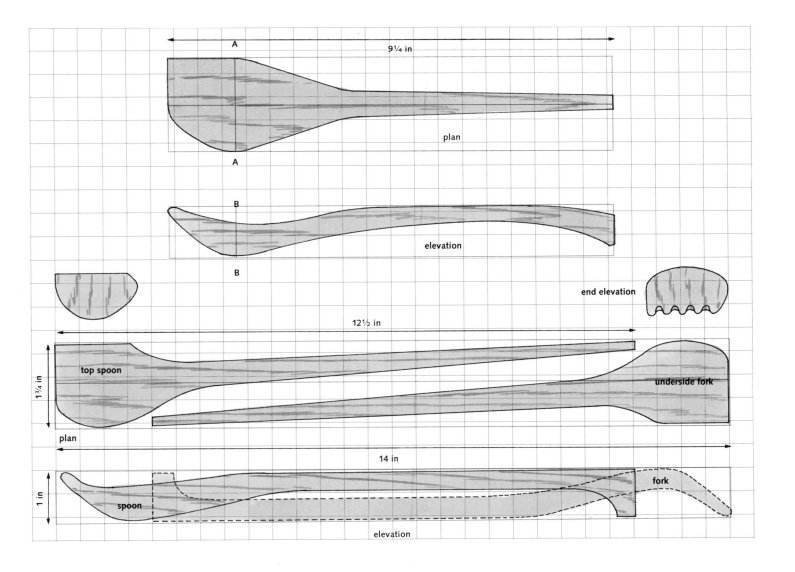

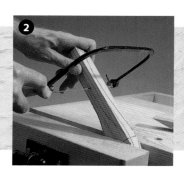

WOODEN SPOON

Method

Following my principle of trying any wood, I used chestnut for the spoon, but this is not a choice I would recommend because the wood has a very marked grain and it can be difficult to make the spoon thin enough at the edge. A closer grained and more evenly-textured wood would be preferable. Many spoons are made of beech, and some of sycamore. I have used holly successfully, and boxwood is excellent, especially for small spoons. The wood for this spoon measured $9\frac{1}{4} \times 2 \times 1$ inches.

The trickiest part to carve cleanly is the bowl of the spoon because, although it is fairly shallow, you need to use your tools from a variety of directions both with and across the grain. Given a sympathetic piece of wood, the handles can often be at least partly shaped with a spokeshave.

Stage one

1 Draw the center line along the top of your wood, down the ends and along the bottom. Draw the line across the widest point of the bowl, $1\frac{3}{8}$ inches from the end and perpendicular to the center line, taking it down the sides and across the bottom. Use these lines to align your plan shape template, and draw the plan shape on top and bottom, keeping the flat side of the spoon the same in both cases. For a right-handed user, the flat side will be on the right, so show this as "top." If you are left-handed, turn the spoon over and mark the other side "top," in effect reversing the template. I like to draw the side elevation as well, even though it will be largely sawn off. The wood is now ready to carve, as illustrated right.

First stage

The construction lines have been drawn on.

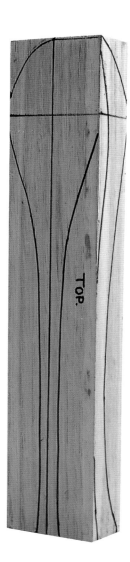

Stage two

2 The first job is to remove the waste as efficiently as possible. To arrive at the plan shape, you can saw just outside the line with a coping saw. This is efficient but slow; it is also fairly difficult to keep to the line on a long straightish run, so leave a generous margin for error. You can, of course, use a band saw or jig saw instead, but in that case you should remove the area beneath the handle and the bowl curve first (step **4**). With the template as a guide, re-draw the elevation you have sawn off. Because some of the side has been cut away, the template will not fit exactly, so go as far as you can around it, and join the lines by eye.

3 The shallow concavity of the top of the bowl is best removed with a chisel and gouge. The mallet is a matter of choice, depending to some extent on the hardness of the wood. Work alternately from the tip and the handle end toward the deepest part of the curve. Tidy up the bottom of the

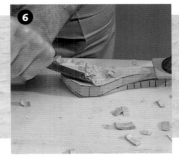

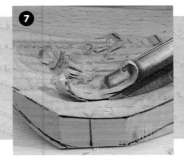

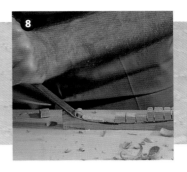

curve with a flattish gouge, carving across the grain from the outside edges to the middle. Re-draw the lines which have been carved away.

④ Saw the waste from the underside of the handle and the curve beneath the bowl, if you have not already done so, with a band saw or jig saw. Your spoon will now appear as shown in the two views below. The center line along the underside of the handle should be re-drawn, and you can then move ahead to step **10**.

Stage three (alternative)

⑤ An alternative way of removing the waste is to make a series of saw cuts perpendicular to the center line, from the outside of the wood to within ⅛ inch of the profile both in plan and in elevation, and then carve off the unwanted wood with a chisel. Work with the grain and do not try to remove too much at one time. When the side waste has been removed and the side elevation of the handle has been re-drawn, your spoon will

look like the illustration below, ready for the bowl and the underside of the handle to be carved.

Stage four (alternative)

⑥ Chiseling the top of the bowl is quicker when there are some saw cuts to stop the wood from splitting.

⑦ You can, if you wish, carve out more of the bowl while the spoon is in this position. The bowl begins with a shallow groove fairly well up the handle, which gradually widens and deepens. Carve alternately from each end toward the

bottom of the hollow. At the deepest part, cut in across the grain toward the middle. I like to use a No. 8 gouge to start with and follow up with the flattest suitable for the particular curve. The bowl of this spoon never gets very deep, but you can vary all the dimensions to suit your requirements.

⑧ Turn the spoon over and carve away the underside of the handle, working with the grain from the end down into the curve. Remove only a small amount with each chisel cut, especially when you are nearing the bottom of the saw cuts.

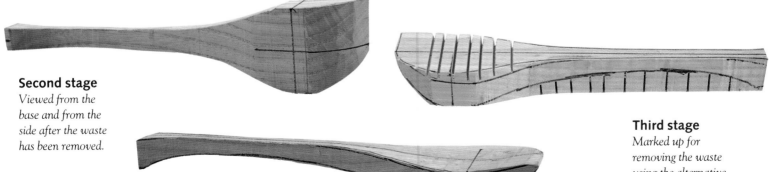

Second stage
Viewed from the base and from the side after the waste has been removed.

Third stage
Marked up for removing the waste using the alternative sawcuts method.

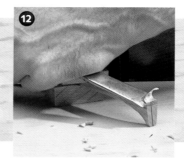

9 Turn the spoon around and work the other way. You will now have roughed out your spoon to the point shown in the views below.

Stage five

10 To shape the underside of the bowl, clamp it underside uppermost, and using a chisel or No. 2 or 3 gouge, work away from the highest point of the bowl toward and along the handle, taking off quite flat chamfers at first. The aim is to make a continuous curve from side to side as well as following the gentler slopes of the side elevation.

11 Turn the spoon around and, still working from the highest point, carve toward the tip. Try as far as possible to keep all parts of the underside progressing together – you will need to move the clamp fairly frequently. On many spoons, a spokeshave is a good alternative for shaping the underside. To use it, strap the spoon with masking tape to a piece of wood just wide enough to hold it. Secure this in a vise, and shave in the directions already mentioned. When you have nearly finished the underside, turn the spoon over and continue to work on the top of the handle and the bowl. Support the handle by placing a small block of wood under the part to be clamped. Round off any corners that might dig in and put a piece of rubber or other padding between the block and the handle.

12 After you have shaped the end of the handle with a chisel or gouge, complete the top of the handle with a few strokes of a spokeshave or cabinet scraper. Finish shaping the inside of the bowl by removing very fine shavings as before. If the wood is close-grained, you can give the spoon quite a fine rim, but if the grain is fairly open, it is best not to make this too thin.

13 A gooseneck scraper is a good tool for the final finishing, because it enables you to hold the spoon in one hand while you work. Make the spoon as smooth as you can, so that it will be easy to clean. I drilled a hole in the end of the handle to hang it up by, but this is optional.

Finishes

The spoon was intended to remain as carved, but the metal of the tools reacted with the wood, creating discolored patches, so these were removed with sandpaper, and the spoon was then left untreated.

Fourth stage
The spoon has been fully roughed out.

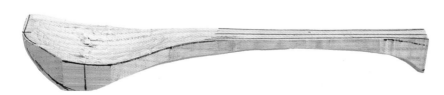

Spoon
Antony Denning

SALAD UTENSILS

Method

The same basic method applies to making salad utensils – in fact, the proportions used here would work equally well for spoons. The wood measured $14 \times 1\frac{3}{4} \times 1$ inches and came from the remains of a 19th-century mahogany bed frame, but almost any hardwood would be suitable. The only way to get both utensils out of this piece of wood was by drawing an asymmetrical design on the wood and then separating the two implements.

Stage one

①Draw the center line down the length of both wide sides of the wood and connect it at the ends. Next draw a line around the wood, perpendicular to the center line, 2 inches from each end. Position your plan template with the straight side of the bowl on the edge of the wood at one end. The tip of the handle should touch the same edge and coincide with the line 2 inches from

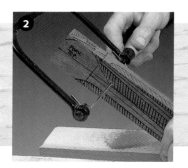

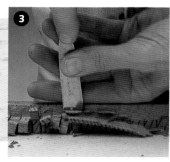

that end. Hold the template in position, with or without masking tape, and draw around it. Repeat the same process with the bowl at the other end of the wood. Turn the wood over and do the same on the other side but with the template inverted. The salad spoon will be the same way around as a right-handed spoon, so choose one of the plan shapes which has the flat side on the right when the end of the handle is toward you, and mark it "spoon top." Turn the wood over and at the other end, with the flat side on the left when the handle is toward you, write "fork top." Turn the wood on one side, position the side elevation template so that its top coincides with the implement on that side, and draw around it. Do the same on the other side.

With a pencil and a straight-edge, draw the center lines down each of the handles on the top and bottom of the wood. You will find the middle easily at the handle tip, but you will need to establish it by eye at the bowl end, or measure across at the point where the handle meets the curve out to the rounded side. Pencil-shade the parts which have to be cut away. You will now have reached the point illustrated below. The shapes at this stage are identical but reversed, so that eventually they can come together like a pair of hands, but you can see how confusing it could be if you left the implements un-labelled.

Stage two

2 Because the two shapes are being cut from one piece of wood, they have to be separated with a coping saw. A jig saw or band saw would make this task easier. Do not worry too much about following the line – there is not a lot of waste to remove, so you can saw

roughly down the middle if you want to. After separating the shapes, draw the side elevations on the sawn sides. Make frequent short saw cuts perpendicular to the center lines to within ⅛ inch of the profiles.

3 and **4** Chisel the waste away from the sides. Keep an eye on the grain to locate any tricky bits that will help you

Second stage
The spoon and fork have been separated and the waste marked for removal.

First stage
The working lines have been drawn on.

establish the best directions for carving different parts.

5 Saw the wedge shape off the underside at the end of the bowl. The Stage Two illustrations below left show the separated spoon and fork, the latter with its sides trimmed, and give you a closer look at the side elevation re-drawn on the fork, together with the short saw cuts. Note that, from the side, although the "bowl" of the fork is thinner than that of the spoon, they both have the same overall depth.

Stage three

6 In the same way as on the wooden spoon, remove the waste from the top of the bowl and the underside of the handle using a chisel or gouge. Carve off quite small pieces and continue to keep a careful eye on the grain. (My old mahogany turned out to have some awkward changes in grain direction.) Bring both implements to the same stage, re-connect any important lines, and clean up the shapes. Your two basic forms will now appear as shown below.

7 Carve the bowl of the spoon, working from both ends and the sides toward the deepest part, as with the wooden spoon. Shave the "bowl" of the fork virtually flat, but with a slightly concave lead-in from the handle.

Stage four

8 Turn the two over and shape the undersides. The fork and spoon are mirror images on this side. Work away from the highest point, either toward and along the handle or toward the tip of the bowl. As with the wooden spoon, your aim is to keep all parts progressing at the same rate. Use your chisels and gouges whichever way up seems to work best at any given moment. The grain of the wood did not encourage me to use a spokeshave, but on a different wood it would be worth trying. The transition from bowl to handle is more abrupt than it was in the wooden spoon: the handle

Third stage
The spoon and fork are both roughed out.

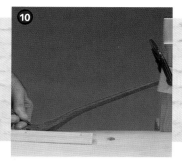

is more or less triangular in section at this point. It merges into the convex shape of the bowl at the sides, but follows the unbroken line of the side elevation top and bottom. The triangular section of the handle becomes more rounded, losing any concavity as it slims down.

9 When shaping the top of the handle, support the underside with a block. The rounding is done with an inverted gouge.

10 It is not always easy to hold these fairly delicate objects, but this proved a satisfactory way when carving the inside of the bowl. The relative flatness across the part of the spoon sitting on the bench prevented it from twisting under pressure. If it had been held with block and clamp as before, the carving of the bowl while it was sitting on the convex underside could have placed too much strain on the handle.

11 Use a 3 mm (⅛ in) No. 11 tool to carve the prongs. You have to do this from both the top and the underside, rounding off between. Begin with the veiner at a low angle, about ⅜ inch from the end, and make four shallow, equidistant grooves to the end on both sides. Start again about ¼ inch from the end, and this time carve around in quickening curves to meet the grooves on the other side. Repeat the action until your prongs reach the required depth, being careful not to make them too deep. Round the ends of the prongs and take off sharp edges.

12 Refine all parts of both utensils with chisels and gouges followed by cabinet scrapers. Use the standard rectangular scraper on the handle and the underside but switch to a gooseneck scraper in the bowl and any other concave parts. It is not unusual to leave utensils of this sort as carved, which is attractive, but in this case I wanted to soften the edges and make them more tactile, so I sanded them with fine sandpaper before oiling. To sand between the prongs, fold the sandpaper around a thin piece of wood or plastic, or a knife blade.

Finishes

The salad utensils were sanded with sandpaper followed by three applications of Danish oil and a hard rub with a cloth. The oil in salad dressings will probably keep the servers in good condition, but if they begin to look dry, re-oil them following the manufacturer's directions. The servers can be hand-washed, but should not be left to soak.

Salad utensils
Antony Denning

It may be cheaper to buy a set of salad utensils, but making your own is more satisfying.

· · · · · · · · · · · · · · · OBJECTIVE · · · · · · · · · · · · · · ·
To design and carve a bowl, relating the inside shape to the outside shape. The bowl
may be decorated or left plain.

BOWL WITH HANDLES

T he word "bowl" conjures up such a variety of shapes and sizes that it has endless possibilities. A bowl can be a restrained, regular shape or a free form. It can be painted, embellished with carved patterns, or rely on the beauty of the wood or its own outline. Carving a bowl is a very satisfying exercise, and likely to meet with approval because it produces a useful object.

DESIGN CONSIDERATIONS

There are several approaches to the design of a bowl. You could dream up a shape and draw it, considering surface decoration as an integral part of the design, then choose an appropriate size and buy your wood. Or you might think first of the bowl's use – perhaps as a fruit or salad bowl – and that will influence your ideas about shape and your choice of wood. Another approach is to look around your workshop for a suitable piece of wood and design your bowl to fit it. Whether your bowl is to be thin and elegant or thick and rugged,

think in terms of a shape that cannot be turned on a lathe.

In selecting a shape for this project, my priority was to incorporate some useful carving techniques, such as those used for the hand holds. I began by noting down the elements that I wanted to include, and then I found a suitable piece of wood. I decided I should like to retain some of the rectangular shape of the wood while cutting into it to reveal a curved bowl shape.

Design drawings will vary according to the type of bowl. If it is a fairly free form, you may only need a sketch with the dimensions written in and a clear indication of how the inside and outside shapes will relate. There is a strong element of formality in my design, so I have made plans and elevations and cut away part to show a section. To maintain the rectangular shape, I have left blocks on the sides and ends. In each corner, between the blocks, the curve of the bowl is revealed. Looked at in elevation, the shapes under the end and side blocks are loosely based upon those seen in boats, where curved shapes also have to fit onto square shapes.

To help get the curves reasonably equal, I have made templates for both the inside and outside shapes (see p. 127). These can be cut from poster board, but I have chosen a transparent plastic used in stonemasonry. This enables you to trace the line directly from your drawing with-out the intermediary of carbon paper or tracing paper. As so often in carving, the drawings and templates are there to help you create the shape you want, but they are not your masters and may be abandoned as soon as you feel confident without them. A slavish copy will lack vitality, and it is rarely necessary to follow a drawing precisely.

PLANS

Using the drawings below and on the next page as a guide draw the plans and elevations full size (see pp. 19–20).

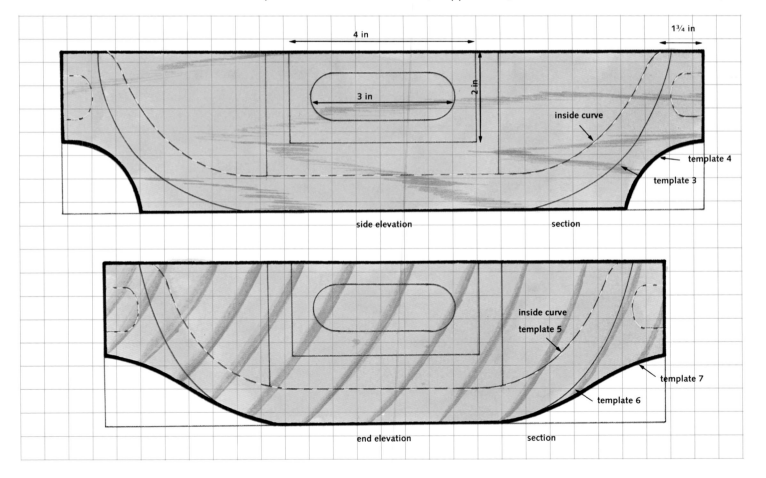

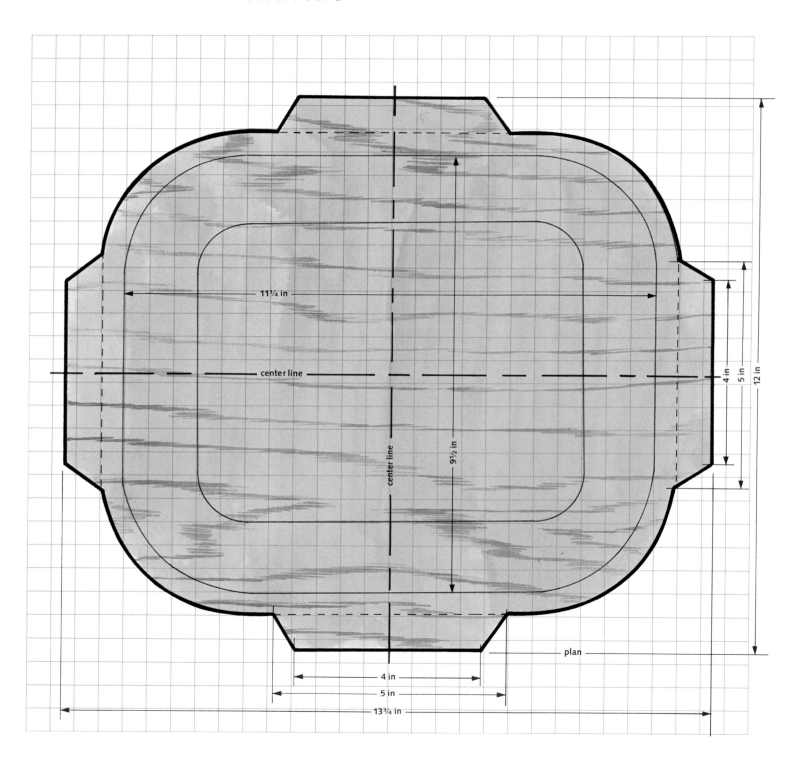

11¼ in

center line

center line

9½ in

4 in
5 in
12 in

4 in
5 in
13¾ in

plan

TEMPLATES

Trace the outlines for the templates from the plans and
elevations and transfer them to thin poster board (see p. 20).

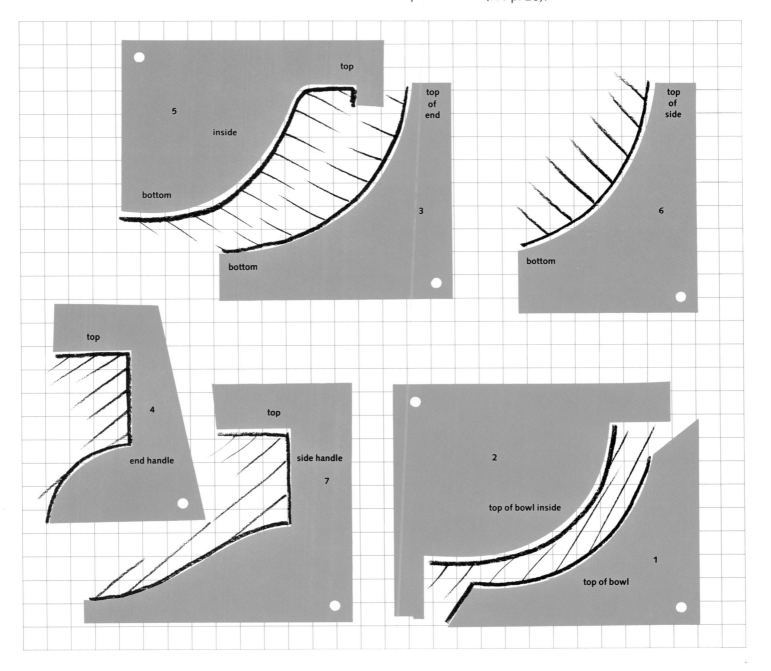

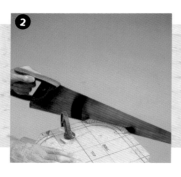

METHOD

Bowls can be made of virtually any wood, but for food use you should choose a non-toxic hardwood. It is always wise to check with the lumber yard that the wood is suitable for your purpose. Chestnut was the choice for this bowl, in a piece measuring 13¾ × 12 × 3½ inches.

Stage one

① Draw the construction lines on the top surface of the wood, take them down the sides and then draw them on the bottom. Next draw in the details of the handles and the profiles of the inside and outside of the bowl. Pencil-shade clearly any parts which are waste and can be cut off right away. This completes the first stage, as illustrated below right.

Stage two

② With a saw, cut off the corners perpendicular to the top surface. Keep the line of your saw cut just outside the perimeter of the bowl.

③ Now make some saw cuts perpendicular to the original side line of the wood (the outside line of the side handles). Cut across the grain to reach the perimeter of the bowl at points just outside the sloping ends of the side handles. Then cut to arrive at similar points for the end handles. The line to follow here is the dotted line across each end handle.

④ Use a chisel to carve away the waste. Work with the grain or across it: on the edges of the side handles it may be easier to carve with the grain, but when chiseling the flat plane at the perimeter, you may have to change direction on different sides. On the edges of the end handles, you would have to work outward to go with the grain, and as

First stage

All the construction lines have been drawn and waste material indicated.

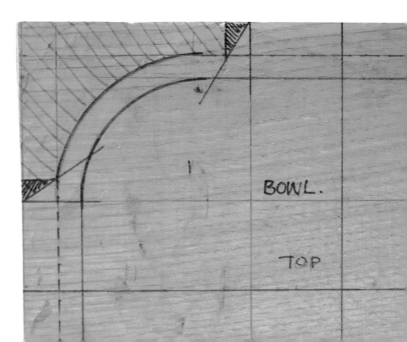

BOWL.

TOP

there is not much room to do this, it is easier to carve down across the grain. You will now have reached the second stage shown below right.

Stage three

5 To set in the curves of the profile at the corners, carve vertically down across the grain for about 1 inch. Start near the side handles and work around to the end handles, finishing with fairly thin tangential shavings close to the final line.

6 Turn your bowl over. The wedge shapes under the end handles can now be sawn off, but those under the side handles are easier to remove with a large gouge, after which they can be planed or chiseled flat. Again be sure to establish the best direction for carving. It will probably do no harm if you split off a piece of wood at the outset – in fact, this can be a deliberate way to speed things up, provided you are careful – but you don't want to tear the wood as you near the final surface.

7 When all the wedges have been removed from under the handles, begin rounding the corners with a large gouge and mallet. Keep the bowl bottom side up and carve around toward the top side. As this is a three-dimensional curve, you will need to work from its center in a series of radiating lines, straight in plan but following the curve of the elevation. Begin some way from the center in order to cut away the bulk of the waste. At first, the area will hardly be rounded, but bear in mind all the time the shape you are aiming for. This process has been likened to peeling off the layers of an onion until you reach the layer you want. As you get nearer to the final shape, start each cut with your tool at a very low angle, gradually increasing it as you follow the curve until you are carving almost vertically downward. Stop before you reach the top side.

8 Try your template against the curve from time to time to see how it is progressing. It is common to feel a bit nervous

and to think you have cut too much away, only to find that you have not gone nearly far enough. Work around the bowl so that all the outside parts are reaching the same stage of development.

9 Using a No. 8 or 9 gouge, carve the concave curves under the end handles most of the way across the grain from one side, and then come in from the other side.

10 You can carve with the grain, following the drawn line, where you find it easier. The S curves under the side handles are much gentler, so remember to carve them in the direction which you earlier found best for that part. Use your templates to check all these curves at different points.

Second stage
The plan shape has been roughed out.

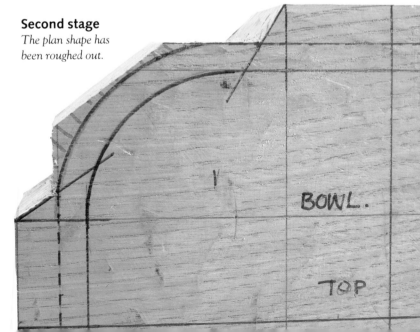

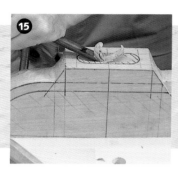

11 There is a slightly concave transition from the convex curves of the corners to the handles which should be carved at the same time. When carving this, you also straighten the edges of the curves under the handles. The illustration below left shows the underside with just the side handle at the top to be completed.

Stage four

12 Continue to refine the outside of the bowl by carving thin slivers off the low ridges between gouge cuts and finishing with scrapers. Here a gooseneck scraper is being used on the junction of convex and concave surfaces. The final smoothing is often done after the inside has been carved to the same degree of completion, and so Stage Four ends with the underside in an almost finished state, as shown below.

Stage five

The next two jobs can be done in either order. Normally I would carve the four handles, and the lowered rims between the handles, as consecutive operations, but for demonstration purposes the two processes are shown alternately.

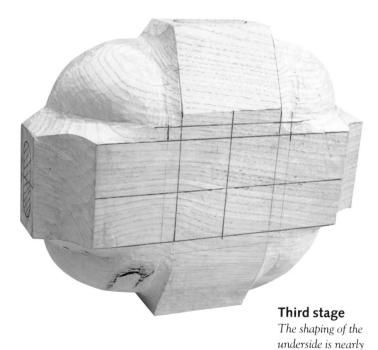

Third stage
The shaping of the underside is nearly complete.

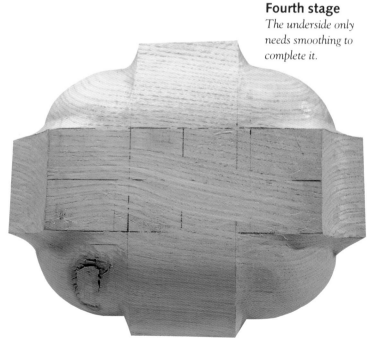

Fourth stage
The underside only needs smoothing to complete it.

13 The tops of the handles are set slightly above the rim of the bowl, so measure 3/16 inch down from the top surface and draw a line around the corners at that level. Using a veiner or parting tool, carve grooves on the top surface of the bowl, just outside the lines that continue the sloping edges of the handles. Carve the grooves in several stages, gradually reaching a depth just short of the line you have drawn. Unless the grain of the wood suggests the opposite, carve the grooves by the side handles inward and those beside the end handles outward. It does not matter how far inside the bowl the grooves start or finish.

14 Carve around the top, with the grain, using a chisel or flattish gouge, such as a No. 2, held at a low angle and keeping above your line. Maintain your tool at an angle across its width as well as its length, and you will be able to concentrate on cutting a clean line on the outside of the bowl. When you near your line, cut inward from the edge

to level it off to at least the width of the rim. Re-draw the lines which show the thickness of the rim.

15 To scoop out the side handles, hold the bowl on its side in a vice. You can use a straight or salmon bent gouge, No. 8 or 9, about 3/8 inch wide. Work from each end of the handle alternately. Make the first cuts some way in from the ends and work back toward them, carving toward the middle with a scooping movement and gradually increasing the depth. Carve the ends of the insides of the handles almost vertically to start with, and then make a quick curve, keeping most of the length an even depth. You can test this with a depth gauge. The tops and bottoms of the scooped-out handles (the sides in this position) can be finished with a chisel.

16 Now turn the bowl around in the vice so that an end handle is uppermost. A bent gouge is the best tool to hollow this handle, and it should be very sharp. Start in the middle

and scoop wood out to a reasonable depth. Work toward one end, then the other. Repeat the process until you have reached the full depth. Unlike the side handles, where you can carve vertically down into the wood, you need to make the sharp edge of your blade scoop upward from below at the ends. That is, you aim to carve outward, which is not as difficult as it sounds once you have cut to a good depth in the middle.

17 When all the handles have been hollowed out, you can turn your attention to the inside of the bowl. There is a lot to remove, so use large gouges, working alternately from each end, starting the cuts close together but gradually working back toward the ends and opening up the middle. Keep well in from the sides at this stage. Start with straight gouges, but when it becomes difficult to follow the inside curve, switch to a salmon bent gouge. It is a good idea to carve one end out nearly to the full depth, working back from the

middle to the end, and then to turn the bowl around and work back to the other end in the same way. Gradually carve the sides outward at the same time. You can often carve the sides down from the top across the grain, following the inside curve in your mind, but watch carefully to make sure that you are not tearing the wood. If it is not cutting cleanly, change direction. Well before you reach the final surface, you will have discovered how your wood behaves and will know which way to carve the different areas. As with the outer profile, check the interior curves with a template from time to time. As you near the finished shape, you will be carving increasingly thin slivers, so it will be easier to stop and change direction when necessary.

18 and **19** A straight gouge will remove fine shavings on the steep end grain, but would dig into a curved surface, where a long bent gouge is needed.

20 A scorp is a useful alternative to a salmon bent gouge, because it is one-handed, enabling you to hold the bowl with the other hand.

21 The tops of the handles need a curve on the inner side where they turn down into the bowl. Carve the side handles with a chisel or gouge, working with the grain along the length of the handle and taking off ever smaller shavings to create a rounded edge. Carve the end handles using a No. 2 gouge. Follow the curve by starting with the gouge almost flat, bringing the angle upward fairly rapidly and ending with it almost vertical. Work across the handle from one side to the other, making a succession of similar movements. You will probably have to do this several times.

22 Now put a similar curve on the inside of each corner, starting near the end handles. Begin with a movement like that used on the end handle, but as you come around the curve gradually switch to carving along the length as you did with the side handles. A back bent gouge can be helpful here, but is not essential. You will almost certainly find it easier to use the gouge the right way up on the parts nearer to the end, but inverted on the straight sides.

23 Rounding the outside of the rim is more straightforward. Invert your gouge and work from the side handle, with the grain, around to the end, carving fine chamfers as you did on the side handles and gradually rounding the sharp edge.

24 Concave curves are carved on the junctions of the handles with the top of the rim. In the case of the side handles, start at the outer edge with the gouge on its side just touching the top corner of the handle. As you push toward the inside of the bowl, gradually increase the depth of your cut while simultaneously twisting your gouge through 90° so that it ends the right way up. The aim is to take very little off the outer part of the handles but to have a smooth transition from bowl to handle. It is best to do this in several fairly gentle stages. For the end handles, you do the carving in reverse: starting from the inside, with the tool the right way up, you take the maximum off and gradually decrease, while twisting the gouge, so that you end at the top corner shaving off nothing and with the gouge on its side.

25 If you want a smooth surface, a final scraping with a gooseneck scraper is a good way to achieve it.

Finishing

The whole bowl can now be finished. If you want it to be smooth, use scrapers, but if you prefer to leave faint tool marks, take fine shavings off with gouges. The flat surfaces of the end handles are most easily sanded, but the side handles can be planed or scraped smooth. A plain bowl can look lovely simply scrubbed clean, but will usually benefit from a protective treatment, especially if it is to be used frequently. This bowl was wetted on the outside to raise the grain slightly, allowed to dry, and finished with three applications of Danish oil. It would be possible to give the grain more prominence by lightly sandblasting the surface.

"Barge Bowl"
Antony Denning

———

The finish brings out the grain of the chestnut.

PROJECT

8

To carve a pictorial relief in a realistic style with a plain background.

RELIEF PANEL

A relief carving lies somewhere between a painting and a fully three-dimensional object. The depth of carving can vary enormously, from virtually three-dimensional high relief, called *alto-rilievo*, through a medium depth, or *mezzo-rilievo*, and low or bas relief, known as *basso-rilievo* – to something hardly more than drawn relief called *relievo-schiacciato*.

Though modeled rather than carved, the bronze door panels of the Baptistery in Florence by Lorenzo Ghiberti (1378–1455) are excellent examples of this mixture of reality and illusion and show the whole range, from almost completely rounded figures in the foreground through every depth to background details which are virtually drawn in perspective.

Though woodcarvings can display a similar variety in a single panel, it is just as common to find a whole panel in low or medium relief. The lower the relief, the more you have to distort, or adopt the devices of drawing and painting, to create an illusion of depth. In many relief carvings, however, it is not the intention of the carver to create a realistic picture. Decorative panels on old four-poster beds, cupboards and chests, bench ends, and pulpits have motifs carved on a plain background. The diversity of subject and treatment is enormous, and the ability of the carvers equally so, but even carvings which are comparatively crude are often delightful.

DESIGN CONSIDERATIONS

Designing a panel is just like planning a painting, and you can, within reason, adopt any style you like. Here the carver has chosen to carve a still life of a basket of fruit on a table. The style is realistic. The two planes of the table and the wall behind are very simply suggested. The elliptical shapes for the basket are drawn as they would be for a painting. The basket texture adds interest and contrasts with the rounded shapes of the fruit.

Remember that it is the shadows which will show the forms and textures, and so a sketch model is invaluable. It will not only give you a picture of the highlights, shadows, and textures, but will also provide you with an opportunity to work out the depths to which you will carve the different parts. You will also be able to spot any changes that are necessary to improve the composition. Drawings and models are part of the design process and may need occasional adaptation. As always, consider them as starting points or steps along the way, not to be reproduced exactly.

PLANS

Divide some paper into squares and enlarge the drawing to actual size (see pp. 19–20). You will use this to prick around or trace (stage one, steps 3 and 4).

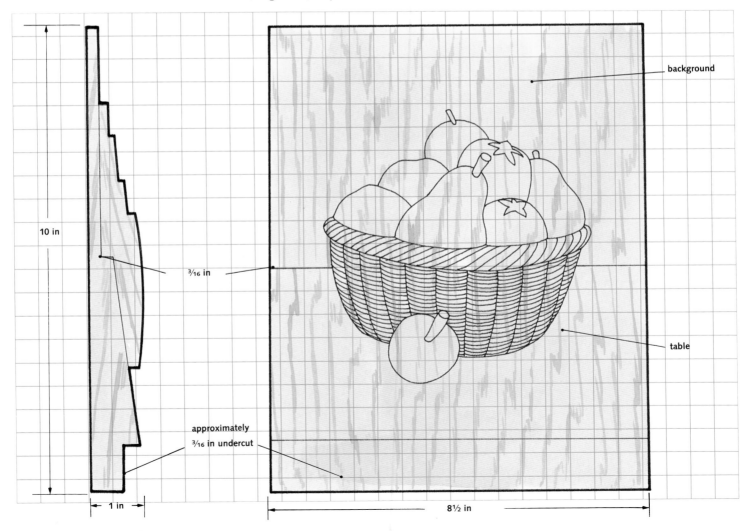

10 in

³⁄₁₆ in

background

table

approximately
³⁄₁₆ in undercut

1 in

8½ in

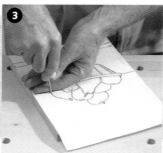
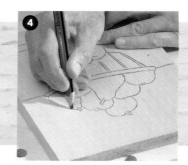
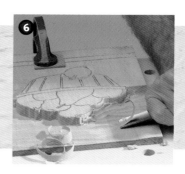

METHOD

For this panel the carver chose basswood – the favorite wood of the German master carvers of the 16th century – but many woods have been used for work in relief, two much used but very different being pine and oak. The dimensions of the wood are 10 × 8½ × 1 inch.

Stage one

①Make an actual-sized sketch model, so that you can transfer measurements directly and easily as you carve.

②Plane the wood, so that your drawing will show up more clearly.

③ and ④ Transfer the drawing to the wood by pricking through the paper with a pointed tool such as an awl, and pencil in the lines. Alternatively, use carbon paper. Your panel will now appear as illustrated right, with the sketch model alongside it.

Stage two

⑤ Before starting to carve, draw on the sides of your wood the lines of the sections of the flat background, the sloping table, and the under edge of the table.

⑥Carve away the background to just above your line with a 13 mm (½ in) No. 6 gouge. The early stages of a carving provide the ideal opportunity to get to know your material, so try the gouge in different

First stage
The drawing has been transferred to the wood (right) from the drawing which was the basis for the sketch model (left).

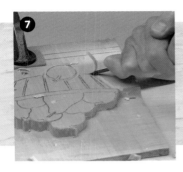

directions to see how the wood behaves. Note that there is a ³⁄₁₆ inch step at the back of the table which catches the light, thus emphasizing the line and helping to create the illusion of depth.

7 Make a shallow gouge cut around the outline of the basket and fruit.

8 Carve the sloping surface of the table top; stop just above your line again to leave some wood for later work.

9 Set in the profile of the fruit and basket, keeping your chisels and gouges perpendicular to the original surface. You have now reached the point illustrated below.

Stage three

10 Begin carving the fruit by taking it down in flattish steps. The model is essential for establishing the relative depths of the different pieces of fruit. Use a strongly directional light source, such as an adjustable reading lamp, to light your carving; put your sketch model beside your work and compare the two. You should also carve

the convex curve on the basket at this stage. Your panel will now look like the illustration below. Notice how the directional light is already beginning to make the piece look three-dimensional. The overlapping of the forms increases the illusion of the depth, and as the basket takes shape, the apple in front of it appears to be thrust forward.

Second stage

The profile has been set in and you can now begin to establish depth and detail.

Third stage

The basic forms have been established.

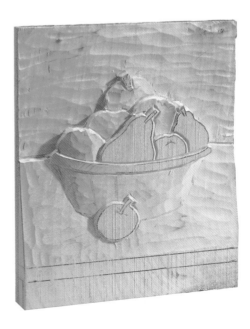

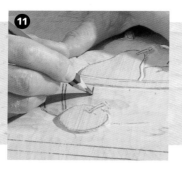

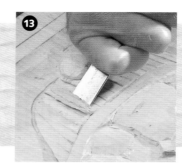

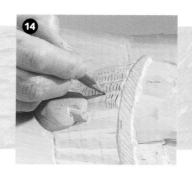

Stage four

11 Draw the detail on the basket carefully, because when it is carved, it will play an important role in expressing the form. The lower the relief, the closer it will be to a drawing.

12 and **13** Continue work on the fruit and carve the undulations of the basket. The carver paused at this point to consider his carving critically against his sketch model and original drawing. He decided there were some modifications to be made. First, he lowered the back of the table to improve the composition. Then he decided that some of the fruit looked out of scale, so he re-drew it. Carve these alterations to complete Stage Four, as shown right. Compare that illustration with the picture of Stage Three to see the modification to the table level, and with the photographs of steps **12** and **13** to note the dramatic difference that directional light makes to the modeling.

Stage five

14 Draw in the texture detail with a pencil. This will give you a clear impression of the finished basket and provide guidelines to follow when you are carving the fine gouge cuts. Take the pencil lines around the form of the basket to convey an illusion of deeper relief and help you imagine the solid form as you carve. Pencil in the features on the fruit around stalks and calyxes.

15 Replace the pencil lines with fine gouge cuts. Keep the solid shapes firmly in mind and take the gouge right around, almost as if you were making a three-dimensional piece (see p. 18).

Look critically at your carving again using a directional light from different angles. You will probably have to do some more modeling of the fruit. Smooth the background by making the gouge marks less coarse. The Stage Five illustration below shows the techniques you can adopt to achieve a greater

Fourth stage
The composition has been adjusted and work has begun on the detail.

Fifth stage
Concentration on detail and perspective has given the carving greater depth and subtlety.

sense of perspective. Note the penciled X above the top apple which the carver has used as a "vanishing point," aiming the gouge cuts on the table top generally in its direction. The sizes of the gouge marks can also lend depth, working on the principle that marks close to the viewer appear larger than those farther away. The cuts on the table, though shaved to a fairly subtle texture, still act as converging lines, leading the eye into the composition, whereas the background marks form a broken pattern that remains unobtrusive. Arrange the cuts either horizontally or vertically to be restful to the eye.

Stage six

⑯ Carve away the area beneath the edge of the table, making a step of about ³⁄₁₆ inch, to create a strong shadow. Finish the fruit with a texture of small, shallow gouge cuts. Make the texture on the apple in front of the basket a little more pronounced and under-cut it very slightly around the

edges to create the shadow that will cause it to stand out against the basket. You will now have completed the panel. Notice the extent to which the shadow under the table edge adds to the three-dimensional effect, and the little details, like the slight hollowing of the stalk ends, which give sparkle to the carving.

Finishes

The panel could be treated with color or given a natural wood finish as here. It was brushed with three coats of clear shellac over 24 hours. After drying thoroughly for two days, it was rubbed down with 0000 steel wool and polished with good-quality furniture wax.

Relief panel
Peter Clothier

The subject is reminiscent of a still-life painting.

. . . . **OBJECTIVE** . . . .

To design and carve a frame of simple construction with applied decoration that follows a pictorial theme.

MIRROR FRAME

A picture frame should complement the picture it encloses, but a mirror frame can almost be a picture in itself, with you, or any other viewer, becoming part of the composition. Mirror frames come in all shapes and sizes, and the degree and types of decoration are as numerous. Some are made with enough wood to enable the entire frame to be carved as one piece, often very elaborately. Such a frame is time-consuming to make, but the principles of construction are basically the same as those in this project.

Here, the frame itself is very simple, and ready-made elements and carved features are applied to it. The carving is in fairly low relief, but different in character from that of the relief panel (p. 134). As the figures have no attached background, they can be "back cut" to make them more three-dimensional. This method of applying items to a simple background can be used in the design of other objects, such as a firescreen or even a relief sculpture in its own right.

DESIGN CONSIDERATIONS

The first task is to choose a theme. Having toyed with ideas of mermaids, owls, and caryatids, I decided on circus clowns, because they can be as distorted as you like, saving you the problem of making them realistic.

In this project you can ignore true scale and perspective. Imagine a circus and clowns. Here, the big top is represented by the frame, and the clowns stand on each side of the mirror. The mirror space needed to become part of the scene, so it was conceived as an entrance. The clowns were given a platform supported by two plinths on which to perform. The circus has to move, so it was provided with wheels. The poles link the roof of the big top and the canopy above the mirror to the platform. The plate at the base is a ground for everything else to stand on. The pennants add a festive touch to the top. First envisaged as elaborately carved shapes, they were finally resolved into more appropriate simple triangles. The clowns needed a linking element, so I imagined them juggling and throwing

TOOLS AND MATERIALS

For the carving:
- Basic toolkit
- Coping saw
- Newspaper or cardboard
- White woodworking glue
- Old blanket or other soft material
- Plywood
- Basswood
- Beech

For the frame:
Woodworking tools, including
- Saw
- Plane
- Drill
- Chisel
- Screwdriver
- Nail set
- Awl
- Marking gauge
- Steel ruler
- Craft knife
- Try square
- Clamps
- Screws
- Masking tape
- Sandpaper
- Wood (see cutting list)
- Useful power tools if available: jig saw or band saw, plane, drill

CUTTING LIST

PREPARED PINE	Width	Thickness	Length	Quantity
Allow a little extra on the lengths when ordering	in	in	in	
1 Sides	5½	1	27	2
2 Cross pieces and tent roof	5½	1	23	3
3 Plinths	5½	1	5½	2
4 Base plate	3¼	1	24¾	1
5 Platform	2½	¼	24	1
6 Trim on edging of tent roof	1¼	¼	24¼	1
7 Side pieces for No. 6	1¼	¼	1⁹⁄₁₆	2
8 Ruffle of canopy over mirror opening	1¼	¼	14	1
9 Backing piece for No. 6	⅝	⁹⁄₁₆	23¾	1
10 Backing pieces for No. 7	⅝	⅜	1	2
11 Backing piece for No. 8 (cut off from No. 5)	⅝	¼	14	1
12 Ends for No. 11 (cut off from No. 5)	⅝	¼	1¼	2
ANY SOFTWOOD				
13 Ready-made molding for sides above platform	⅞	⅜	20¾	2
14 Ready-made molding for sides below platform	⅞	⅜	5½	2
BASSWOOD (measurements of thickness for sawn wood not preplaned)				
15 Clowns	4½	1¼	17½	2
16 Wheels (can be cut from one piece approx. 1¼ in thick)	4½	⅝	4½	2
17 Pennants	1¼	½	2¾	3
BEECH				
18 Turned balls	1			12
HARDWOOD DOWELS				
19 Poles for tent	⁹⁄₁₆		21	2
20 Axles for wheels	½		1¾	2
21 To peg roof to top of frame (optional)	⅜		3½	2
22 For canopy poles	¼		16¼	2
23 For pennants	¼		3¾	3
24 For beech balls	¼		1⅜	11
25 For lynch pins	¼		1⅛	2
THIN PLYWOOD OR HARDBOARD				
26 Backing for mirror	12⁵⁄₁₆		16³⁄₁₆	1
27 Mirror	12¼		16	1

The dowels have to be adjusted to fit, so treat the lengths as approximate. Check before cutting to fit your frame.

balls to each other, and of course some balls are dropped. While sketching, the face of one of the clowns looked vaguely moonlike, so he became the moon clown, and inevitably his companion had to be the sun clown. Hence the Circus of the Sun and the Moon. Having dreamed up the concept, the practical designing begins.

The mirror has to work as a whole, but it is helpful to think of it as two separate phases which will be brought together. The basic frame is just a construction job, and the most important drawing for it is an accurate front elevation. Draw it actual size if possible; otherwise, draw it carefully to scale and mark in the actual dimensions. It may also be useful to show hidden detail, such as the rabbet for the mirror, with dotted lines. First, decide upon the size of the mirror and the width of the wood for the frame. With these, you can draw the basic rectangles. Add a shallow triangle to the top for the roof of the tent. Two squares of the wood width will make the plinths. A simple decorative edging is needed on the roof of the tent to make the illusion work, and this has to be placed in front of the frame so that the tops of the poles will fit behind it. The canopy over the mirror is treated in the same way, but has slimmer poles and will protrude less far. The platform can be of quite thin wood and will project in front of the plinths. The base plate is the same thickness as the frame, but narrower. The clowns are to occupy the spaces on either side of the mirror, so the wood for them can be narrower, but here they have been made as big as possible. The turned beech balls, which were bought, will be arranged and attached after the clowns are in position.

This exploded diagram (below) clearly shows how the mirror was put together.

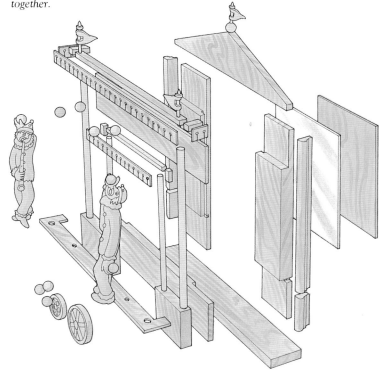

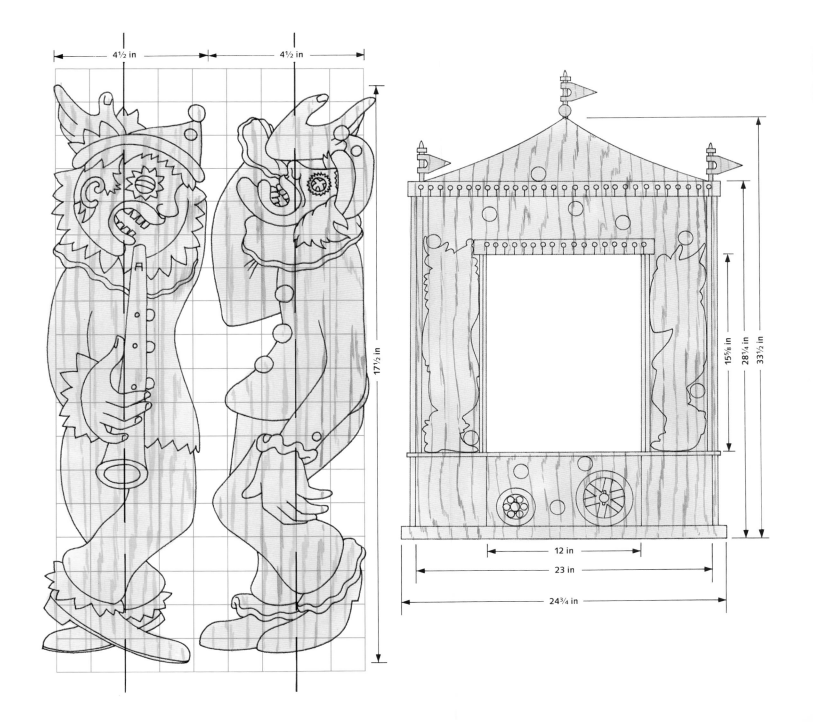

METHOD

You will need ordinary wood-working tools for the frame, and clamps to hold it square when assembling. Corner clamps would be useful, but the wood is too wide for some models. The frame is made with basic lap joints (see p. 45), but note that these are larger than is normally recommended, so they are screwed as well as glued. The expansion and contraction of the wood over the full width can impose quite a strain, and you could decrease the area of gluing by cutting a rabbet (see p. 45) about 1½ inches wide in the back of the cross pieces, and making the side pieces correspondingly shorter. From your drawing, make a cutting list of all the items you will need, as shown on p. 141.

In this example, pine without knots was used for the frame, and basswood for the clowns, wheels, and pennants. The poles are an unspecified hardwood, probably ramin. Ready-made softwood molding is used on the sides above and below the platform. The turned balls are beech. The axles for the wheels are cut offs of beech dowel rod with lynch pins of ramin.

You may like to begin by making the frame (see p. 150), or start with the carving, as shown here (Stages One to Eight). The two are brought together on p. 150 (*Assembly*).

Carved features
Stage one

① Both wheels can come out of a 4½ inch square taken from the same length of wood as the clowns. Draw concentric circles on the square for the hub and the inner and outer parts of the wheel, and mark the center lines of the six spokes, as shown below.

② Cut around the circle with a coping saw. You could use a jig saw or band saw if you prefer. Draw the spokes and shade the areas which will be pierced. Mark a line around the rim dividing the wood in half. You have now reached the point illustrated below, with the double-thickness wheel ready for separation.

First stage

The working lines have been marked on the wheel.

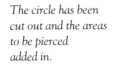

Stage two

③ Hold the wheel on edge in a vise and saw halfway through. Loosen the vise and roll the wheel 90°. Then, with the saw cut away from you, tighten the vise and saw the third quadrant. Turn the wheel again, and slip some poster board into the saw cut before returning it to the vise with the fourth quadrant exposed.

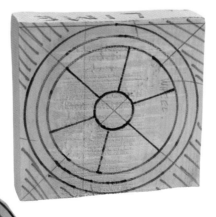

The circle has been cut out and the areas to be pierced added in.

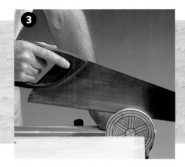

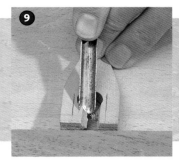

④ Decide how far to reduce the smaller wheel. Re-draw the wheel accordingly and saw around the circumference. Drill six ½ inch holes between the spokes, and another through the center for the axle. In the larger wheel, drill as many ¼ inch holes as you can between the spokes.

❺ Clean out the spaces with chisels and gouges. Use a No. 8 gouge to make a shallow cut around each wheel about ¼ inch inside the rims. Change direction where appropriate to allow for the grain. Make another cut around the hub, then gently pare the spokes in between to leave them as simple squared shapes. Mark the axles with an awl about ⅜ inch from the ends and drill ¼ inch holes for the lynch pins. Glue them in place. Your wheels are now complete, as shown below right.

Stage three

⑥ Draw the construction lines for a pennant on the wood, and drill a hole ¼ inch diameter, from top to bottom, as illustrated below right.

⑦ Round the end that is to be parallel with the flagpole, work inward from top and bottom with your gouges. Taper the top, bottom, front, and back to the point.

⑧ Drill a ½ inch diameter hole through from front to back with its center about ⅝ inch from the pole end.

❾ Clean out and tidy up the U shape with chisels and gouges. The pennant is complete, as illustrated below. Make the others in the same way.

Stage four

⑩ Draw the clowns first, preferably actual size. Square up some tracing paper and trace them. Cut out the tracings to use as templates. You may find you need these to be stiffer – here, stonemasons' orange template material was used.

⑪ Square up a modeling board large enough for both clowns (or two smaller boards). Align the lines on each tracing with those on the board. Draw the outlines of the clowns.

Second stage
Completed wheels with lynch pins.

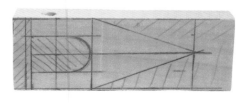

Third stage
Pennant drawn onto wood.

Completed pennant.

⑫ Make a bridge using cut offs of clown wood for the supports, and a strip of wood long enough to span the width of the clowns comfortably: say, 5½ inches between the supports. Build a clay model of each clown, and check the depth with the bridge. The sketch models of the sun clown (left) and the moon clown (right) are shown right. Originally modeled in clay, they were cast in plaster of Paris for transportation.

Stage five

⑬ Square up the wood in the same way as before. Align and draw around the templates. Shade the wood to be removed. You have reached the point illustrated right, showing the moon clown.

⑭ Cut around the profile with a coping saw, keeping just outside the line. A band saw or a jig saw can be used if available. Alternatively, make frequent saw cuts almost to the outline perpendicular to the edge of the wood, and carve away the excess with a chisel.

⑮ Clean up the profile with chisels and gouges. The sides should be perpendicular to the top surface. Draw the detail by copying a square at a time from the tracing.

⑯ Make a backing board for each clown by gluing some newspaper or poster board to a piece of plywood larger than the clown. Glue each clown to this surface, using as little

Fourth stage
Sketch models of the sun and moon clowns.

Fifth stage
The moon clown outline has been transferred to the wood.

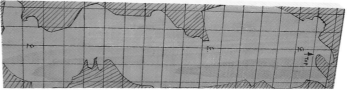

glue as possible. The paper or poster board enables you to separate the backing boards from the clowns when carved, but saturation with glue will make this difficult. You can now use clamps to hold the work.

⑰ and ⑱ Expert carvers try to reach the desired shapes with as few cuts as possible by choosing a tool with the right sweep and thereby gaining clean, crisp forms. This obviously takes experience, but is a good goal to have in mind from the start. In the early stages, carve away as much as possible with large chisels and gouges: the roughing in, roughing out, or shaping process. Work right-handed and left-handed if you can to avoid constantly moving the clamps. However, wielding a mallet with your "wrong" hand can be awkward without practice.

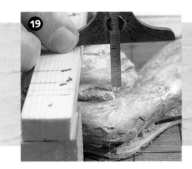

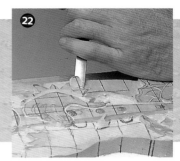

19 , **20** , and **21** Take depth measurements from the model and check the depths you have carved on the wood. The illustrations right show your carving toward the end of this stage, with the moon clown partly shaped and the sun clown slightly more advanced. Note that the three finger holes in the musical pipe have been drilled to mark their positions.

Stage six

22 When establishing the positions of details such as the cuff ruffles, stab in vertically with an appropriately shaped gouge, then remove the chips by coming in parallel with the plane against which they will eventually sit, but do not try to reach the final depth at this stage.

Fifth stage
The shapes have been roughed out and the detail started.

23 Some details will, at their highest points, fall upon the original surface of the wood, so be careful, particularly on the heads. For instance, carve the ear of the sun clown so that you can see how much to remove around it. If you start carving the mouth, you can get a clearer picture of how much deeper you will have to make the saucer shape around that side of the head to get the best effect.

24 and **25** Work around the inner line of the lips with the corner of a sharp gouge. Then with the gouge at a shallow angle, take some wood off the teeth.

26 When you are leaving one part for another, re-draw the details to help you keep the final appearance in view.

27 Work over the whole head carving the three-dimensional shapes – for example, the curves on the hats, heads, and faces, and the hair masses.

28 The eyes are bulbous shapes, so stab a circle and carve the saucer shape under the eyebrows, and inward from the nose and mouth. Carve the eyeball with a rounded gouge as near as possible the diameter and curvature of the eye. Start in the middle of the eye with the gouge almost flat and, working with the grain, push rapidly, raising the handle until you are carving straight down; in other words, you follow the curve of the eyeball with the cutting edge. Then do the same in the opposite direction. Details such as the "petals" around the eye and the slit through it can be carved when you are happy with the modeling of the nose and mouth. The illustration right of the sun clown shows the carving at this stage. Note how the details of the head are clarifying and nearing completion. The left hand has been opened up and made thinner. The carving is more finished at the top, so the next stage is to bring it all to the same state.

Sixth stage

The sun clown is now at quite an advanced stage, with much of the detail added.

Stage seven

29 Carve the hand holding the musical pipe before finishing the pipe itself, in case you want to give yourself more depth for the hand. This is an area where several layers have to be suggested without much depth of carving. Create the roundness along the length of the pipe with an inverted gouge. Be careful to make sure that the sides of the pipe continue in straight lines on each side of the hand. The opening below the mouthpiece is rectangular and the lower part slopes up and into the "sharp" edge (look at a recorder if you need to check on this).

30 When carving the pants, think of the structure of the leg inside, especially where the bone comes close to the surface – at the kneecap, for example. The same applies to the sleeves and arms.

31 Re-draw the welts on the roughed-out boots and the details of the ankle ruffles. Use a V tool initially to carve the welts, then round the boots into them. Consult the

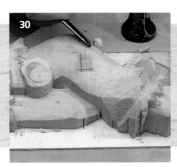

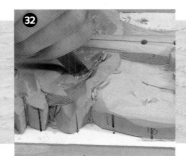

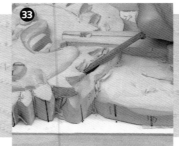

sketch models and the moon clown illustration for this stage (right) to get some idea of the different treatments for the tops of the ruffles. When these are satisfactory, carve the petals on the sun clown's ankle ruffles and shape the bottoms of the pants to meet them. The moon clown's ruff, cuffs, and anklets all have tapering gouge cuts from the outside in; make the concave shapes first, then around the tops.

32 and **33** The sun clown's ruff is similar. Where the petals around his face overlap the ruff, carve vertically down on each side, then come in parallel with the ruff to cut out the chip. If necessary, use a skew chisel to reach into the corner. Employ the same technique wherever you find similar

Seventh stage

The detail on the moon clown needs further refinement.

shapes. In some areas, you can make fairly long shaping cuts – on the sun clown's tunic, for instance – but in a carving of this sort, you need to do a lot of modeling of forms with a flat gouge, such as a No. 2, taking off quite thin slivers as you near the final surface.

34 Details such as the buttons and the bobbles on the hats are carved in the same way as the eyes; though the curve of the buttons is flattened over the top, but tight and quick around the sides. You are now ready to separate the carvings from their backing boards.

Stage eight

35 Some parts are now fairly fragile, so be careful. You can wet the cardboard or paper, but try not to wet the carving. Let the cardboard soak up the moisture so that it tears apart easily. Pry each carving off the board and scrape as much residue as you can from the underside.

36 Turn the clown face down on a soft surface, such as a discarded blanket or a piece of

bubble wrap, and back carve the underside to create a more rounded quality. You can remove quite a lot behind the left hand and knee of the moon clown, but in other places – his right arm, for example – you have to be more subtle, because the carving is already quite thin. The aim is to free the figure from its background and make it appear three-dimensional, so carve the minimum required to achieve this. Always leave at least a small edge perpendicular to the upper surface. This can be rounded if appropriate, but avoid knife edges. Where the sun clown's hat overlaps the canopy, it has to have ½ inch carved away, so bear this in mind from the start. Make final adjustments to both clowns when you can check them against the frame.

37 The whole surface of each clown is finished with tools. It would be very difficult to use sandpaper on such complex shapes.

Frame

① Prepare all the parts of the frame, but do not drill the holes in the platform yet. Glue and clamp the plinths onto the bottom cross piece with the grain of the plinths running from top to bottom, and put two screws in each from behind.

② Assemble the basic frame of two sides and top and bottom cross pieces. When the corners are square, glue and clamp them. Insert screws from the back. Glue and nail the base plate in position: use finishing nails and drive the heads below the surface with a nail set.

③ The fringed edgings of the tent roof and the canopy over the mirror need backing pieces to thrust them forward. Attach the top backing piece in position with glue and a few brads, so that it overlaps the top edge of the frame by ¼ inch. Attach the side backing pieces in the same way.

④ Glue the roof of the tent so that it sits on the top edge of the frame within the recess. Attach it with screws about 2 inches from each end.

⑤ Lightly mark the position of the top of the canopy, and glue and nail the backing in place. Be careful to align the long central piece correctly before adding the mitered ends.

⑥ The platform sits on the plinths, but is also set into the side pieces both on their front and side surfaces. Using a try square, mark a line across each side ¼ inch above the top of the plinths, carrying the lines down the outsides as well. Saw to a depth of ¼ inch on these lines, chisel out the waste, and try attaching the platform. The inner edge of the platform forms the main part of the depth of the front edge of the bottom rabbet, so make sure the line is right. While it is in place, mark the positions of the holes to take the tent poles and the smaller canopy poles. The outer edges of the tent poles are aligned with the outer edges of the frame, and the inner edges of the canopy poles are ¼ inch in from the reveals of the mirror opening. (Unless your

carpentry is highly accurate, leave the marking and drilling of these holes until after the basic frame has been constructed.) Take the platform out and drill the holes.

⑦ Re-assemble the platform together with the poles. If all is well, take out the poles, and glue and clamp the platform in position. Tap in a brad on each side where it will be hidden by a clown's shoe, but keep the clamps in the mirror opening until the glue has well set. Drill ¹⁄₁₆ inch holes near the tops of all the poles for brads. Put a little glue in each hole on the platform, and push the ends of the poles in. Make sure the pin-holes are facing outward, then tap in brads to hold the tops.

⑧ Drill a few holes for brads in the side moldings, and glue and nail them in position.

⑨ Mark the strips of wood for the canopy fringe and the big top roof edging. The ³⁄₁₆ inch holes are drilled at ¾ inch centers on a line ½ inch from the lower edge. Mark the holes at the center and work out.

When you have drilled the holes, countersink them. Make a saw cut perpendicular to the edge of each hole, and chamfer the edges with a chisel. Turn the strip over and clean up the back.

⑩ Glue and clamp the canopy fringe and then do the same with the tent edging.

⑪ Attach the mirror in the frame and temporarily nail the backing board in position.

Assembly

① Mark on the template two points on each clown where the wood is thickest. Transfer to the frame. Drill screw holes through the frame and countersink on the back.

② With the frame horizontal and the clowns in position, arrange the wheels and 11 balls. Mark centers on frame. Drill ¼ inch holes through frame for balls and to ³⁄₈ inch depth in balls. Drill right through 12th ball. Glue 1³⁄₈ inch dowels in holes.

③ With frame vertical, drill ¼ inch holes ½ inch deep for pennants. Drill ½ inch holes for axles in frame. Drill ¼ inch holes 1 inch deep down the middle of a ⁹⁄₁₆ inch dowel. Saw three ¼ inch rings off dowel. Smooth rough edges. Point the ends of the pennant poles and glue rings just below points. Glue pennants just below rings. Glue 12th ball just below one pennant. Try pennants in holes and adjust length if necessary.

④ Decorate all pieces separately.

⑤ When the paint is dry, assemble (gluing or screwing where appropriate) as shown on page 143).

Finishes

The original plan was a varnished natural wood finish, but as the carving developed it became apparent that color would make it more interesting as well as suiting the theme. Keeping the color thin on the tent would allow the wood grain to show through, so Japan color thinned with mineral spirits was used. The wood was first sealed with a coat of clear shellac, and the paint was protected with flat varnish. The colors were the complementaries yellow and violet, with white and black.

Circus of the Sun and the Moon

Antony Denning

. . . . **OBJECTIVE** . . . .

To produce a decorative carving designed to appear three-dimensional, but intended for display against a wall.

SIGNS OF THE ZODIAC

There is a wealth of weird and wonderful creatures from mythology, ancient traditions, and systems of divination like astrology which can provide inspiration for carvings. The result could be described as a form of three-dimensional illustration. Folklore and early beliefs can be fascinating in themselves, and visual material is plentiful in sources such as astrology books and medieval bestiaries. Your imagination can carry you as far from the original as you choose, or you can invent your own beasts, following the example of Lewis Carroll and others.

DESIGN CONSIDERATIONS

After choosing a creature, carry out any additional research and start making some drawings. I chose the signs of the zodiac because of their endless fascination for so many people, whether skeptical or not. I decided to begin at the beginning of the modern calendar with Capricorn. Sadly, there was no opportunity of returning to Chartres Cathedral in France, where I remembered seeing signs of the zodiac carved on the west portal, so I had to be satisfied with consulting books. One of the oldest known representations of Capricorn is on a Babylonian boundary stone of the 10th century B.C., which shows how ancient it is. Early depictions frequently show a hairy goat from its curved horns to its middle, but with a fish tail. I preferred this version to the plain goat forms because of its mythological character.

If you plan to carve all twelve signs, you should spend some time thinking about the total composition. Traditionally, the signs are arranged on a circular band with the Earth at the center. You could divide the band into twelve similarly shaped segments, each framing one sign. This would impose a fairly strict, but stimulating, discipline on the design and composition of 12 very different signs. After experimenting with various shapes, I designed the Capricorn not to be circular itself, but to fit happily within a circle.

PLAN

Enlarge the drawing onto squared up tracing paper (see pp. 19–20). Number the lines from left to right and bottom to top and indicate the vertical center line. Before you cut it out to make a template, make sure the numbers on the lines are within the drawing.

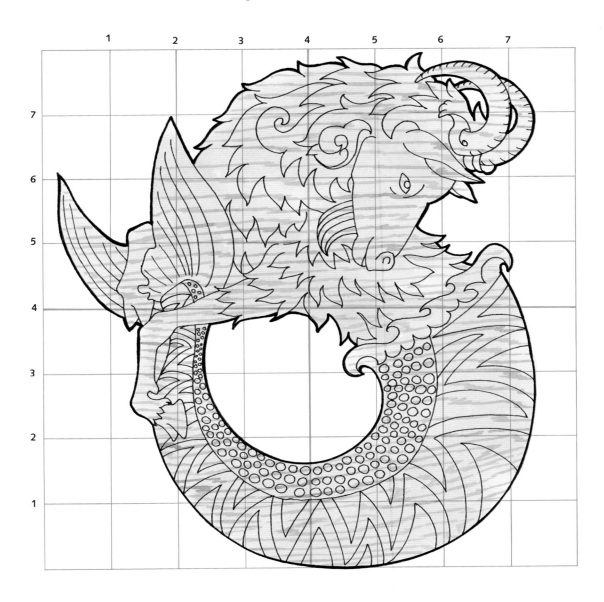

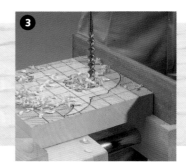
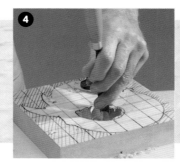

METHOD

There is quite a lot of texture in this carving, so it is better to avoid wood with a significant grain or figure. Basswood was the choice here, in a piece measuring 8 × 8 × 1¼ inches.

Stage one

1 Square up the wood in the same way as the tracing.

2 Align the tracing accurately on the wood and draw around it. Number the lines from bottom to top and from left to right, and mark the center line "CL." Shade the areas of waste wood which are to be removed. You have now reached the point illustrated right (shaded in pen for clarity).

Stage two

3 Make the open part in the middle, speeding the removal of wood by drilling as many holes as you can with a drill or a brace and bit.

4 Clean out the hole with chisels and gouges, carving straight through perpendicular to the surface of the wood.

5 Use a coping saw to cut around the outside profile. This could be done with a band saw. A jig saw would cut both the inner and outer profiles

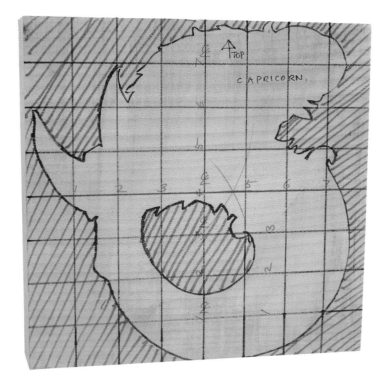

First stage

The working lines have been transferred to the wood. Waste areas are shaded in green.

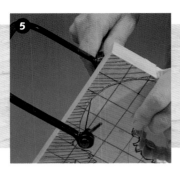

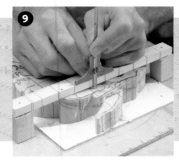

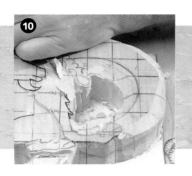

very quickly. Your creature is now fully cut out, as in the illustration below, which includes some of the detail to be drawn next.

Second stage
The shape has been cut out and initial detail added.

Stage three
6 Copy the details, a square at a time, from the tracing.

7 Set up your sketch model under a good directional light, as shown below right, changing the angle of the light source from time to time to help you reassess the forms. This model was made in clay, but as it had to travel quite a lot, it was cast in plaster of Paris and attached to the modeling board. A coat of orange shellac toned down the white plaster and made it easier to see.

Stage four
8 Glue a piece of poster board or newspaper to a board, and glue your carving to it with a sparing amount of white woodworking glue.

9 Use a bridge and depth gauge to transfer measurements from the model to the wood. (A depth gauge can be improvised with a piece of stick or a pencil.) Numbered lines on the wood and model board and measuring marks on the bridge will help you to find the right place.

10 Carve away the unwanted bulky parts, using the biggest tool you reasonably can. In some of the inner areas, you will obviously be restricted, but roughly shape the larger forms to be as bold as possible.

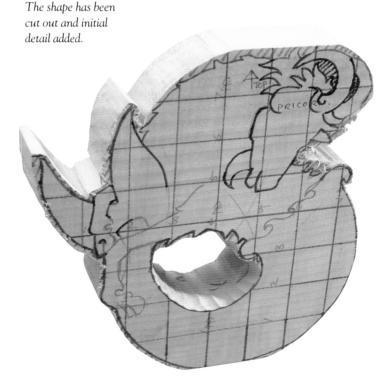

Third stage
The sketch model helps you assess the forms.

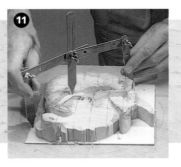

11 Continue taking measurements for as long as you find it helpful. A three-legged caliper can prove useful here.

12 You can easily take the measurements around the edge from the base instead of using a bridge. Remember to pause at intervals and view the piece upright, lit from different directions. Try to keep every aspect moving forward at the same pace. The illustrations below show how the form takes shape during this stage, with much of the detail re-drawn ready for the next phase of carving.

Stage five

13 Carve the shaggy coat, preferably with a fishtail gouge. Make fairly bold cuts straight in, then come in parallel with the surface to remove the chip. You may have to use a skew chisel in the corners. The coat is arranged in overlapping layers similar to irregular shingles on a roof. You will have to shape these more carefully later and tidy them up. Leave the area between the

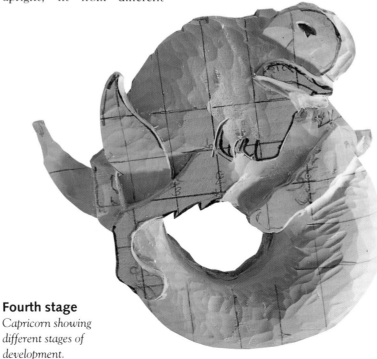

Fourth stage
Capricorn showing different stages of development.

  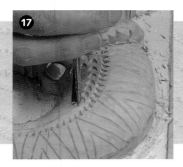 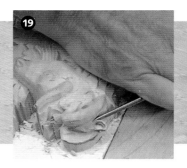

horns for the time being; although attached at both ends, these are quite vulnerable.

14 and **15** The tail fin and outer part of the "fish" are patterned with shallow grooves carved with a V tool.

16 Make the "stripe" down the side of the fish by stabbing fairly gently with a small V tool and removing the chips with a skew chisel.

17 Use the same technique to carve the rounded scales on the inner side of the fish, but with a veiner and a small chisel.

18 Gradually finish remaining areas such as the legs and hooves. Undercut the left foreleg and pierce the space between it and the fish.

19 Carve the space between the horns. You may find it easier to hold the creature upright in a vise to get at these parts.

Fifth stage
Most of the detail has been carved; only a few final touches remain.

Stage six

20 When carving the features on the head, remember that it is the shadows which give depth and form to a carving, so try not to be too finicky with the details. Go over the entire front again, refining surfaces and shapes until you are satisfied with the piece as a whole. Now carefully remove the carving from the board by gently prying it up from different directions with a chisel. Clean any poster board or paper from the back. Place the creature face down on a soft but firm surface (such as an old blanket), which you don't mind damaging, and shape the back. The aim of "back carving" is to make the piece look as though it has been carved in the round, so you need only take off enough to create the illusion. Frequent viewings from the front are necessary to gauge the effect.

Finishes

A decorative object of this kind lends itself to a great variety of finishes, from a simple coating of shellac or oil followed by waxing for a natural wood look, through a range of polychrome treatments to burnished gilding (see Finishing, p. 50). This Capricorn was given three applications of Danish oil followed by a microcrystalline wax polish.

Sixth stage

The front carving has been finished (top). The shaped back is shown below.

Capricorn
Antony Denning

———

The composition of this lively carving is pleasingly harmonious.

PROJECT

11

. . . . OBJECTIVE . . . .
To carve a fully three-dimensional piece, which is visually satisfying from all viewpoints.

CARVING IN 3-D

The subject for your three-dimensional carving could be a human figure, or an animal, bird, or fish. It is probably wise to limit yourself to a single form at first and make more complex compositions later. The carver of this project chose to carve a cat. Some of the objects in other projects – such as the box and the bowl – are free-standing and three-dimensional, but the figurative carving is in relief and has, to all intents and purposes, a best viewing point.

There have been times in the history of art when even entirely three-dimensional sculpture has deliberately had a favored viewing point, as in the work of the Italian baroque sculptor Giovanni Lorenzo Bernini (1598–1680). Other three-dimensional pieces can only be fully appreciated by moving around the sculpture to experience the ever-changing profiles and forms. However, a three-dimensional form, whether or not it has a best viewing point, needs to be carved fully "in the round," so that you can see it from every angle as a complete object

even if some viewpoints are more interesting than others. You can think of the shape as being composed of an infinite number of subtly changing silhouettes (see page 19).

DESIGN CONSIDERATIONS

It is difficult to visualize a creature of any sort from all angles, and though it is possible with a computer, it may not be practicable. A good way to acquire the perception is to do a lot of drawing, but if you want to draw animals from life, they will rarely oblige you by sitting still. I have sometimes solved the problem by going to a museum and drawing stuffed animals, but even then you may not get the view or pose you need. By making a model (see p. 22), you will see more easily if something is not right and can gradually move closer to your imagined carving. By adding and subtracting, and by modifying an angle here or there, you work your way to a satisfactory composition. If possible, use a modeling stand with a turntable; then you can revolve it slowly to see how the shape alters and where it may need improvement.

Archaic sculpture, such as that of ancient Egypt, gives the impression that side views have been stuck onto the front and back views. Later sculpture not only makes the transition from one plane to another more convincing, but also introduces movement. This does not mean motion but changes of direction, like the twisting of the body, or the placing of weight on one foot so that the angles of hips and shoulders alter for balance and create a gentle "S" curve through the figure. If the eye is to be invited to wander around your sculpture, some of these changes of plane are necessary, so put a slight twist in the body, incline and turn the head a little, or do both.

To begin working on the wood, you will have to start with two views – usually the front and the side provide the best silhouettes. You can cut them out and use them as templates.

For this project, the carver made a number of 2 inch-high sketch models in modeling compound (see p. 21), developed the one he liked best, and created an actual-size mock-up, also in a modeling compound. Note, however, that this is still a sketch which will be further developed in the carving. The finished cat will be called a woodcarving by one person, but a piece of sculpture by another. Purist carvers will certainly repudiate the use of rifflers and sandpaper to remove the tool marks and make a softer form. The carver suggests that this could define the distinction: if the tool marks remain, it is a woodcarving; if they are smoothed away, it is a piece of sculpture. The debate could be endless, but what really matters is the piece itself, and however you label it, the process of carving will be the means to the end.

PLANS

Make an orthographic projection of the front and side views using the practical method described on page 22. Cut out two templates.

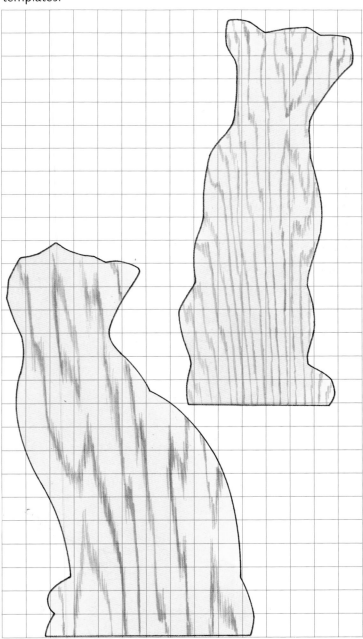

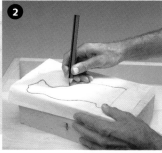

METHOD

Wood with a marked grain or figure could be very successful for this project, but any wood would do. Here the carver has chosen pine from a local lumber yard. The dimensions are $10\frac{1}{2} \times 6 \times 3\frac{3}{4}$ inches. An extra piece is left on to secure the work in a vise. The cat will be 8 inches high.

Stage one

① Make a model like the one below and when you are happy with it, use the method described on p. 22 to create two templates. Draw the base line upon which the cat sits, $2\frac{1}{2}$ inches from the bottom edge, all around the wood.

Stage two

② Use carbon paper under a drawing, or a template, to transfer the side profile of the cat onto one side of the wood. You will now have reached the point illustrated at right. Note the wood below the cat which will enable you to hold it in the vise during carving – an efficient solution to a common problem in three-dimensional work. The block can be cut off when carving is complete, or be incorporated in a base.

Stage three

③ Saw some largish, roughly wedge-shaped pieces from the front and back, keeping outside the line, and then make frequent saw cuts into the line to help prevent the wood from splitting.

④ Cut off the waste wood with chisels, straight across. Use a try square from time to time to check that you are shaving wood off the profile perpendicular to the flat side. You have now completed the third stage, as shown below, with the side profile of the cat going right through the block.

First stage
Maquette.

Second stage
The profile drawn on the wood around the side template.

Third stage
The profile carved straight across.

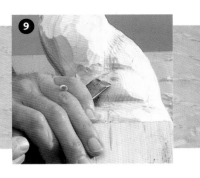

Stage four

⑤ Draw the front profile. A stiff template will be more effective than a paper one on the uneven surface.

Fourth stage
Cut with band saw.

6 Shade to indicate what needs to be removed. Make saw cuts and carve away the waste wood with chisels as you did on the side profile. Alternatively, you can cut both profiles with a band saw, the result of which is shown left. This is much quicker, and if you are careful, you can tape one of the first cut offs back in place and then band saw the front elevation.

Stage five

⑦ The sketch model will be important for general visual reference and for measurement. Draw on the larger shapes and the grid lines which will be useful for measuring. To establish measuring points, mark the model at significant places, such as the tops of the shoulders, with a matchstick or pointed tool. Most particularly, indicate the center line on the model and on the wood. Constant reference to this line will help you keep the two sides even. It will also prove essential when you are taking measurements with calipers

(see p. 18), so re-draw immediately any part of it that you carve away. You will now be at the point illustrated below, which shows the two profiles cut out, together with the model.

Stage six

8 Remove the corners and other bulky areas, using a large flattish gouge, such as a No. 3 or 4, so that you are not tempted to think in terms of

detail. Your aim is to rough out or shape in a rather blocky looking cat with quite flat planes.
9 The whole piece should develop at the same pace, so keep checking that you have reached the same stage all over before proceeding. Take your cat out of the vise from time to time, view it from every angle, and compare it with the model. Though you have no intention of making a slavish copy, these comparisons will

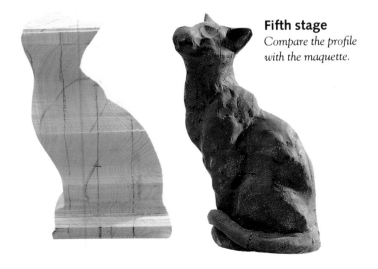

Fifth stage
Compare the profile with the maquette.

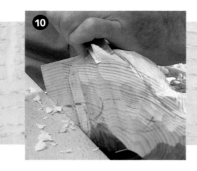

help you see if you are on the right lines. Mark the measuring points on the wood again and relate the measurements to those on the model; in this way, you can quickly establish how much still needs to be removed.

10 Change the position in the vise as often as necessary to get at the different parts. Note how the important center line up the back helps to give a

Sixth stage
The form of the cat has been revealed, but it is still very rough.

strong direction to the carving, and how some details, such as shoulders and ears, are emerging. The penciled cross on the right shoulder is a measuring point which relates back to the model.

Continue carving, measuring, and re-carving until the whole cat form is revealed, even though it may still have obvious gouge marks all over it. Make a saw cut into the block, about 3/16 inch deep, all the way around just below the tail to enable you to "round over" the tail and paws. You are now at the end of Stage Six, as shown left.

Stage seven
12 At this point you can choose one of two different methods of finishing the cat. You can continue to refine the form with smaller gouge cuts, in the same way as the carved panel (p. 134). This will produce a

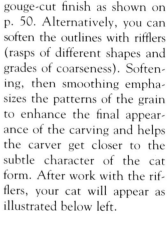

Seventh stage
Rifflers have softened the outline and removed the tool marks.

gouge-cut finish as shown on p. 50. Alternatively, you can soften the outlines with rifflers (rasps of different shapes and grades of coarseness). Softening, then smoothing emphasizes the patterns of the grain to enhance the final appearance of the carving and helps the carver get closer to the subtle character of the cat form. After work with the rifflers, your cat will appear as illustrated below left.

Stage eight
13 Rifflers leave the surface rough, so you will need to smooth it with a succession of sandpapers, from coarse to fine. Make sure you have finished carving, however, before you use any sandpaper, because

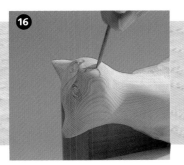

particles left in the wood will quickly blunt your tools. You can create a very smooth surface by wetting the carving with water and leaving it overnight to dry. This raises the grain, which you sand again with fine sandpaper. The carver repeated this process three times before he was satisfied with the finish.

14 Add the details such as eyes and mouth. Draw two faint guidelines to help you: one down the center of the head and nose, and the other at right angles to it through the middle of the eyes. You have now reached the point shown below left.

15 and **16** Carefully carve in the details and carry out any final finishing.

Finishes
The cat was sanded to a very fine grit to show up the grain and given three coats of clear shellac. After thorough drying, it was polished with a furniture wax recommended for antique furniture.

Eighth stage

Seated cat
Peter Clothier

———

A smooth finish enhances the feline appearance.

. . . . OBJECTIVE . . . .

To carve a deeply modeled head in high relief as a decorative object.

CARVED MASK

Masks can be funny, grotesque, beautiful, or hideous; they can take any form, human, animal, or monster; and they can be made of almost any material. In some societies, masks play an important part in religion and magic, and when worn by the priest or his equivalent, they confer great power. Even funny masks can be frightening, because masks not only enable their wearers to alter their appearance and personality, but also to shed inhibitions.

A wooden mask can be made to be worn like any other, but frequently the term applies to a face carved in relief but not hollowed out.

Masks have their roots in our most distant past, and like the carver of this project, who has researched his subject extensively, I find them interesting and powerful. The Green Man, which he has chosen, is similarly represented, entwined with leaves, throughout Europe as far away as Turkey. Considering that he is believed to be a potent if mysterious spirit from a pre-Christian cult, it may seem surprising that he is so frequently found carved on and in Christian churches. This is presumably because the early Church tended to assimilate the traditions of existing religions in a similar way to the Romans, who made the gods and goddesses of conquered peoples the equivalents of their own.

DESIGN CONSIDERATIONS

The Green Man is composed of two elements – the human face and the leaf forms – and the aim is to create a design which fits these neatly into a regular shape. Here, the carver has used a circle, but you might find that another shape suits you better. If you decide to make a hollow mask with pierced eyes, do this in the same way as hollowing the bowl (see p. 128) when the front of the mask is nearing completion.

The degree of realism or abstraction is also a matter for personal choice. Masks tend to have exaggerated features, and although this is not essential, it is worth bear-

TOOLS AND MATERIALS

- Basic toolkit
- Saw
- Board
- Newspaper
- White woodworking glue
- Mineral spirits
- Oak (or any carvable wood)
- Useful power tools if available: band saw. Arbotech Woodcarver and angle grinder for hollow mask only

ing in mind when designing them. The Green Man occurs in many variations, but almost all have an arresting presence. In Germany's Bamberg Cathedral, there is an awe-inspiring stone-carved version in which the entire mask is an acanthus leaf, so subtly designed and carved that it is impossible to determine where leaf becomes face and face leaf. Some portrayals have a naturalistic face peering out from foliage. In others, leaves grow out of face and head and often issue from the mouth as well. The foliage varies in design and type, but the three most popular identifiable leaves seem to be acanthus, oak, and grapevine. You may find it helpful to track down some examples of the Green Man in your local library and note any details of interest.

The most accessible model for your design will be the face you find in the mirror, unless you are lucky enough to have another patient sitter. The leaves can be of any kind. They seldom taste pleasant, but if you sketch them sprouting from your mouth, make sure they are nontoxic. Here the carver has used the acanthus leaf, whose development over many centuries for architectural decoration is one of his interests. His mirror helped him decide how to treat the facial features. He made drawings and a clay model. The drawings need to show the outline shapes of the foliage and the face, and should be actual size. The model, also actual size, will help you to work out the three-dimensional forms that you want. Some carvers like to model the face and then apply the leaves, which is a good way to make the mask convincing.

PLAN

Enlarge the drawing onto squared tracing paper (see pp. 19–20) and cut around the circle to make a template.

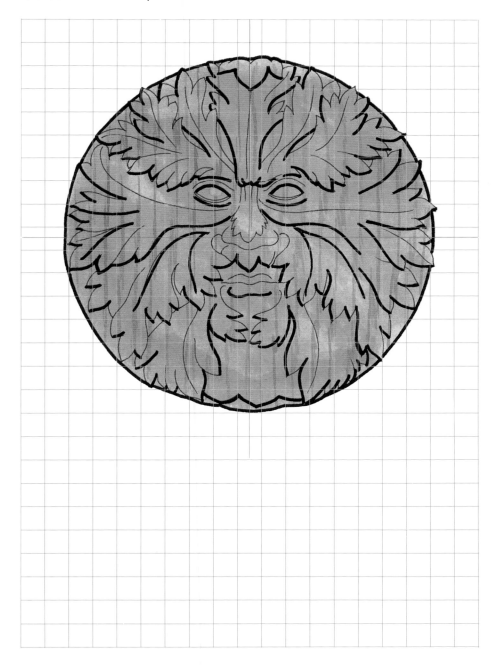

METHOD

The carver chose oak, much used traditionally for carving in England, but any carvable wood would be suitable. Remember that, if you use oak or another hard wood, the bevels on your tools should not be too fine. The dimensions of the piece were 13 × 13 × 2 inches. It was necessary to join two pieces edge to edge, so he planed the edges square and flat, glued them, and clamped them together. He used white woodworking glue, which does not damage chisel edges.

Stage one

1 After doing some rough sketches, make a full-sized sketch model in clay. Notice that the carver has modeled one half more than the other. This is not only because there is a symmetrical balance which makes equal modeling of both sides unnecessary, but also because he is using it as an aid to thought and vision and not to copy. The model will be useful in the early stages of carving for taking measurements and establishing depths. Keep it damp in case you want to return to it to work out an elusive detail before carving it.

2 Make a full-sized working drawing from the model, showing the profiles of the leaves. It is a good idea to have a tracing of this to check against your carving as the work progresses. Bear in mind, however, that once you get into the carving, you will constantly be modifying shapes and making the changes demanded by the translation into wood.

3 Tape the tracing over some carbon paper on the planed surface of the oak and transfer the drawing. Saw off the corners if you wish.

4 Using a white woodworking glue, glue two or three sheets of newspaper to a board quite a lot larger than the oak. Then glue the oak to the paper. This will allow you to remove the finished carving relatively easily without damaging it.

5 Begin carving by stabbing the outlines, using a mallet and large gouges. The eventual aim is to make the edges perpendicular to the uncarved top surface. The profile of the whole object will go straight down to the board, but the inner outlines of the leaves should not be taken down too far at this stage.

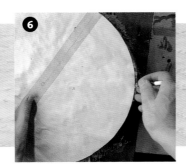

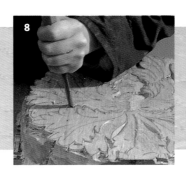

6 Convert the tracing into a simple template by cutting around the circle. Use this to check the overall shape of your carving. This is particularly useful when the carving of the leaves is underway and the lines get lost.

7 Use a bridge and a depth gauge on the model and then on the wood to establish the depths of different parts of the carving. A depth gauge can easily be improvised using a pencil, a nail, or a stick.

8 To start with, the shaping of the leaves and face is rather tentative. You are having to find your way into the carving. Use the largest gouges possible so that you are not tempted to begin carving detail. This is when you get to know the wood and discover the best directions for carving. Use the mallet and large tools for as long as you can. It is a good idea to stop at intervals and prop your carving up where you can step back and look at it. Shine a light at it from different angles. You will now have reached the point shown right.

First stage
The features and leaves are just beginning to form.

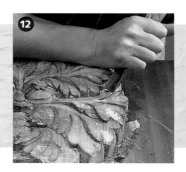

Stage two

9 Try to keep the whole of your carving moving forward at the same pace. Work with or without a mallet, whichever seems better at a particular point. Continue to carve the three-dimensional forms of the leaves and those containing the eyes, mouth, and nose. The illustrations below show stages in the development of these forms. Notice in each case how all the parts of the carving have been brought to a similar state.

Stage three

10 Use calipers or dividers to check your measurements against those on the model for as long as you feel you need to. As the carving progresses, you will rely less on the model, and you are likely to find that the carving itself suggests alternative approaches. Some carvers will always adhere to their original concept, whereas others allow the carving to develop and change fairly radically.

11 The face is the most difficult part, where one cut can change the expressiveness quite dramatically. A mirror is useful here, and making faces at yourself can be a valuable way of discovering how to carve the features. With the leaves, your aim is to impart a feeling of life and growth. In section, the acanthus leaf will have gentle "S" curves running through it. These may end in a backward curve or a pronounced forward curl – as happens top center of this mask – but notice also how many of the small lobes have a slightly hollowed upward turn at the tip. This helps to convey the springiness of a growing leaf.

12 Wet the surface of the carving from time to time with mineral spirits. This evens the tone, allowing you to see the whole piece clearly, and lubricates the tools, making the cutting easier.

Second stage
Mask in different stages of development.

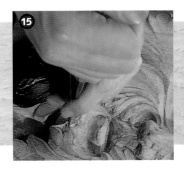

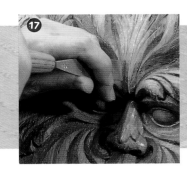

13 Even when the carving is well advanced, you need to look at it critically and pencil in any changes, however small.

14 If you are going to hollow out the mask, it is advisable to do this before carving the fine detail. Use the same method as for hollowing the bowl, but be more gentle, and keep a folded blanket or other soft padding under the front of the mask while you carve. The best way to hold it in my experience is with a cobblers' strap (see p. 39).

15 If your mask is designed to be hung vertically, it is worth carving it upright in the final stages. You will now have reached the point illustrated in the two views right. Notice the emergence of detail, in the eyelids, for example.

Stage four

16 Carve in details such as the veins of the foliage, which follow the leaf shapes and help to emphasize the curves of their forms.

17 The central vein projects and has to be cut cleanly along the edges to make it crisp.

Third stage

View the mask vertically from the front and from the side.

18 and **19** Undercut the edges of the leaves on the perimeter and wherever else it is desirable to add crispness to the carving, such as under the top curl.

20 Clean up all the lines around the eyes and the edges of the leaves and the mouth. You will find that fishtail gouges are particularly useful at this stage.

The illustration below shows the carving virtually finished. The mask is a satisfying whole, with the leaf forms composed to fit happily into a circle. All the forms flow in and out of each other, and even though he is "camouflaged" by the leaves, the face of the Green Man is a forceful presence.

Finishes

Masks are often painted, and the Green Man is no exception. The treatment is often very naturalistic, but it can be finished in whatever manner you feel is appropriate. The finish used is described on p. 51.

Fourth stage
The mask is virtually finished.

Green Man mask
Ross Fuller

Leaves and features unite to form a powerful presence.

INDEX

ACKNOWLEDGMENTS

The author would like to thank Rachel Bridge for reading the manuscript and typing the book.

Quarto would like to thank all the woodcarvers who contributed work for inclusion in this book. Additional picture credits:

La Belle Aurore 10r; Central Art Archives, Museum of Contemporary Art, Helsinki 91; Peter Clothier 1; e.t. archive 6, 8; The Henry Moore Foundation 9r, 16b; National Trust Photographic Library/J. Whitaker 71, 13l, 16t;

Visual Arts Library 7r; "Voivre" from Hargreaves New Illustrated Bestiary by Joyce Hargreaves, published by Gothic Image Publications, 1990 17; Martin Wenham (alphabet) 106–7, lettercarving on jacket.

Key: b = bottom, l = left, r = right, t = top of page

Quarto would also like to thank the woodcarvers who provided projects, techniques, and information for the book:

Peter Clothier 22 (making a template), 88–93, 134–9, 160–165; Lucinda Denning 74–81; Antony Denning 82–7, 94–103, 114–123, 124–133, 140–151, 152–9; Ross Fuller 47–9 (defects), 51–2 (finishing), 166–173; Michael Lewis 39–40 (holding the work and improvised devices), 42–3 (trial blanks), and for demonstrating at

photographic sessions; Clare Timings 52–3 (gilding); Martin Wenham 104–113.

Quarto would particularly like to thank **Alec Tiranti Ltd.** (Reading and London), and **Tilgear** (Cuffley, Herts.) for supplying tools and equipment for photography, and **General Woodwork Supplies** (London) for supplying tools for the jacket photography.

Index by Dorothy Frame